# FATHER TO SON

# FATHER TO SON

## How To Teach Your Children About Sex And Pre-marriage

## A CHRISTIAN TEACHING HANDBOOK

*by*
Roddy L. Couts

Unless indicated otherwise, all Scripture quotations are taken from the King James translations out of the original tongues.

Copyright © 1988
Roddy L. Couts
All rights reserved.
Printed in the U.S.A.

ISBN 0-914903-49-7

Library of Congress Catalog Card Number 87-063226

**Published by
Destiny Image Publishers
P.O. Box 351
Shippensburg, PA 17257**

## DEDICATION

This book is dedicated
to the Church for

The perfecting of the saints

The work of the ministry

The edifying of the body of Christ

# Acknowledgments

This book would not have been possible without the leading of the Holy Spirit. He was with me every step of the way.

As such, I give honor to my Lord Jesus Christ for the words contained herein. I thank Him for using me to pen it.

I also thank the many ministers the Holy Spirit spoke to me through in the writing of this book. This group includes:

> The many evangelists broadcasting Christian television and radio programs to the Washington D.C. area.

> Traveling evangelists, pastors and teachers also ministering in the Nation's Capital.

> The comprehensive teaching programs offered at the Rhema Christian Center Church also in Washington, D.C.

And finally I thank my dear son Christopher Todd, who received the initial teachings.

May the words of *Father to Son* — words of the true and Living God — be engrafted into the fertile grounds of your heart. And may the grace of our Lord Jesus Christ be with each of you.

In the Name of Jesus, Amen                         Roddy L. Couts

# CONTENTS

Dedication
Acknowledgements

## Volume I  Spiritual Preparation For Teaching

| | | |
|---|---|---|
| Chapter 1 | How I Overcame & Taught My Son | 1 |
| Chapter 2 | Why Fathers Should Teach Their Sons | 7 |
| Chapter 3 | What & When To Teach Your Son | 15 |
| Chapter 4 | Why The Name of Jesus Overcomes | 27 |
| Chapter 5 | If You're Not Sure You're Saved | 47 |
| Chapter 6 | How To Use This Book | 53 |
| Chapter 7 | How To Teach The Lessons | 59 |

## Volume II Lessons On Sex

Sex Lesson No. 1
    Your Spiritual Foundation In Jesus

Sex Lesson No. 2
    The Basic Facts of Life

Sex Lesson No. 3
    How Sexual Temptations Come

Sex Lesson No. 4
>Jesus — The Role Model For Overcoming

Sex Lesson No. 5
>Overcoming Peer and Other Pressure

Sex Lesson No. 6
>How To Follow God's Map

Sex Lesson No. 7
>Becoming More Like Jesus

## Volume III Lessons For Pre-Marriage Counseling

Pre-Marriage Lesson No. 1
>Marriage Is Ordained By God

Pre-Marriage Lesson No. 2
>Duties of the Husband & Wife

Pre-Marriage Lesson No. 3
>Sexual Relations

Pre-Marriage Lesson No. 4
>Duties of Parents & Children

Pre-Marriage Lesson No. 5
>Priorities & Problem Prevention

Pre-Marriage Lesson No. 6
>How To Follow God's Map

Pre-Marriage Lesson No. 7
>Communications & Problem Solving

Closing Comments
>A Marriage With Vision

# FATHER TO SON

---

## Volume I

### Preparations For Teaching

# Chapter 1

# How I Overcame & Taught My Son

I had a problem! What do I tell him? How do I tell him? But the good news is that I overcame and taught my son about sex.

But then another problem as I was writing this book! A voice would say words like, "How can you, of all people, have a book like this published?" And the good news is that I overcame again and wrote the very book you are reading.

What I want to share with you in this chapter is how I overcame to both teach my son and to write this book. I pray it will be a blessing, especially to those of you who may not feel your history is "good enough" to teach your sons or daughters about sex.

**My Son Was Turning Into a Man**

My fourteen year old was developing a moustache and facial hair. His voice was getting deeper and I'm sure he had grown 4 inches over the summer. Not only that, he was starting to care more about his personal appearance.

And he was starting to care more about girls, too. In fact, a few girls were starting to phone him "just to chat." Others were even stopping by our house to see him! What? When I was a boy, girls were never permitted to call guys, let alone visit them! What was this world coming to, I thought to myself!

And the telephone! I had never heard him talk in a voice like that! When that macho, "Hey, what's up" he gave to his buddies turned into a soft "Hi", there was no question that a girl had just called. And I would occasionally hear words like, "I like...what do you like? Oh you do! Really!" And his voice would get softer and softer as the calls got longer and longer.

**My Wife Wanted Me to Talk With Him**

While I was observing all this from a traditional man's point of view, "My kid is turning into a man!", my wife got concerned and asked me if I had talked to him about the "facts of life". Oh, no! Why did she have to ask me that question? She knew what the answer was. Of course I hadn't talked with him. For one thing, I didn't know what to say or how to say it.

After agonizing about it for a while I thought, "Why not buy a book on the subject. Surely someone has written a book for fathers in this predicament." So I went out to purchase a book; but to no avail. I couldn't find a book to tell me how to teach my son about sex. What a predicament! While my son was on one hand wanting me to talk to him about sex, and my wife on the other hand pushing me to do it as soon as possible, there I sat with nothing to say. At least so I thought.

**So I Told Him What God Had To Say!**

And then it finally came to me (I heard the Holy Spirit). Why not find out what God would have me tell him! If I tell him out of my worldly wisdom, what good could come of that!

Besides, I had been learning how to apply the word of God in other facets of my life. I had even been healed of ulcerative colitis, a so-called 'incurable disease', by doing what the Bible told me to do. If the Bible had the answers to sickness and disease, surely it had the words of wisdom on sexual morality.

So I searched the scriptures to find words that would help me teach my son. And as I found them I would tell him. Not only would I tell him what they said, I would tell him where they came from. While he could reject me, I knew he would not reject the word of God. It is the only unchanging authority that exists.

So over a period of several weeks I taught him about sex — what kind of sex is permitted by God and what kinds are not. Sometimes we would chat in the TV room, other times in his bedroom. On one occasion we even talked over lunch in a fast food restaurant when no other customers were around.

One day I asked him the reasons kids give for having sex before marriage. And what an answer! He said it was because they didn't want to be clumsy at it when they got married.

**I Promised to Tell Him More Before Marriage**

This really concerned me. My son was walking around hearing a worldly logical though scripturally sinful argument for premarital sex. And I could just see it beating against him every day. I also knew it was a time bomb I had to defuse.

So what did I do? I told him that I would be teaching him the details of sexual intercourse before he got married. I also told him that I would counsel him on any sexual concerns he had after he got married.

You should have seen his face light up. I could see a burden lift from him right in front of my eyes. It was almost as if he was carrying the weight of the world on his shoulders. I truly feel that this promise was the most important part of the teaching. And I was relieved to find out in the Book of Titus that God actually commands us to teach them how to love their wives.

**Should I Write the Book?**

Even as I was writing this book, someone or something was suggesting I not have it published. And though I knew the book was a calling from God, another voice was saying not to do it. Fortunately, I found out what the things really were and who was saying them. And I found out from the word of God.

The first thing was **condemnation!** Was I under condemnation! I had not been without sexual sin in my life, and I was living in a world obsessed with sexual sin. So the voice was saying, "How can you write a book like this?"

The second thing was **pride.** I had learned about Christian faith as a child. But over the years, the "I can do all things through Christ which strengthens me," had been 'rounded off' to "I can do all things." Jesus was left out of the picture.

As a result I was operating on self-will and pride and feeling 'at risk' to be embarrassed by the book. The voice was then saying: "What if your teaching doesn't take with your son?" What if your son lives his life as a sexual sinner? "What would people say?"

And the third thing was **confusion.** Between the condemnation and the pride, I was really confused. But why, I asked myself? Our God is not the author of confusion, as it is written:

> **1 Corinthians 14:33**
> *For God is not the author of confusion, but of peace...*

So it could not be God bringing my past against me or playing up potential embarrassment to stop me—it had to be Satan. And what did I do then? I took a closer look at the scriptures. And there I found that **my past** sins had been condemned, but **I** was not condemned with them. As it is written:

> **Romans 8:1-2**
> *1 There is therefore now no condemnation to them which are in Christ Jesus, who walk not after the flesh, but after the Spirit.*
>
> *2 For the law of the Spirit of life in Christ Jesus hath made me free from* **the law of sin and death.**

This meant that I, being a Christian, was delivered from condemnation; God not only would not, he could not condemn me for it. If he were to condemn me, that would make him a liar. And if I felt condemned, it was only because I was holding on to condemnation at Satan's suggestion. And did I let go in a hurry!

Then, I used a scripture out of Proverbs to overcome the pride problem. More accurately, the scripture purged it from me. I found out that Satan was subtly using pride to try and keep me from doing the Lord's work. But more importantly, I found out that God hates pride. As it is written:

**Proverbs 6:17-18**
*These six things doth the LORD hate: yea, seven are an abomination unto him: A proud look, a lying tongue...*

And I also found one reason God hates pride. As is also written in Proverbs:

**Proverbs 16:18**
*Pride goeth before destruction, and an haughty spirit before a fall.*

So this meant that if I let pride get in the way of God's work I was going to fail. But I was sure of my calling to write the book. And being sure of the calling, the following scripture made it absolutely clear that I should proceed:

**2 Peter 1:10-11**
*10 But he that lacketh these things is **blind**, and cannot see afar off, and hath forgotten that **he was purged from his old sins.***

*11 Wherefore the rather, brethren, give diligence **to make your calling and election sure:** for if ye do these things ye shall never fail.*

So I met the qualifications: I was certainly not blind. God had given me the vision. I was purged from my old sins. I knew my calling. So I simply had to do what God told me to do. And I would not fail.

**Condemned ... Prideful ... Confused ?**

If you feel condemnation, embarrassed or just plain confused, I am here to tell you that God has no special admiration or respect for me just because he called me to write this book. He respects obedience to his word.

God's lack of favoritism to persons or discrimination against persons is made very clear in the early days of the Church. It was then that He had Peter, a Jew, go to the house of a Gentile named Cornelius.

While the Jews detested non-Jews, viewing them as dogs, Peter did as he was told saying, the following to Cornelius:

**Acts 10:34**
*Of a truth I perceive that **God is no respecter of persons.**"*

After preaching the Gospel to them, Peter saw the Holy Ghost fall on Cornelius and the other Gentiles in his house.

**Involved In Sexual Sin?**

Don't worry if you discover you are involved in sexual sins as you read this book. God is good. He makes provisions for forgiveness and healing in his word for any of us who sin.

God will forgive you just as He forgave Solomon, a man who angered him by the many strange women that turned his heart from Him. The four steps you must take to are as follows:

**2 Chronicles 7:14**
*If my people, which are called by my name, shall:*

1. *Humble themselves, and*
2. *Pray, and*
3. *Seek my face, and*
4. *Turn from their wicked ways,*

*Then will I:*

1. *Hear from heaven, and*
2. *Will forgive their sin, and*
3. *Will heal their land.*

**My Prayer**

So in writing this book, I want to give you the revelations that God has given to me on how to teach my son. It is my personal prayer that you and your family be blessed by using God's word to teach the sanctity of the most intimate relationships we have in our physical lives.

In Jesus name, Amen.

# Chapter 2

# *Why Fathers Should Teach Their Sons*

There are a number of reasons fathers should teach their children about sex. They include the following:

- God says so,
- Your son wants you to teach him,
- You are the priest of your house,
- Your son will be blessed, and
- Your son will not be destroyed

This chapter takes a look at each of these reasons from the standpoint of the scriptures. Also included is the example of Eli, an Old Testament priest who failed to train up his sons in the way they should go.

As you'll see when you read about Eli, you don't want to be judged as he was judged!

**God Says So**

Not only is it common sense for us to teach our children, the word of God says it is our responsibility. In the book of Deuteronomy, God speaking through Moses says:

**Deuteronomy 6:6**
*And these words, which I command thee this day, shall be in thine heart: And thou shalt teach them diligently unto thy children...*

God said it. That should settle it. That's why we must teach our children. But God continues telling us how often:

**Deuteronomy 6:7**
*...and shalt talk of them when thou sittest in thine house, and when thou walkest by the way and when thou liest down, and when thou risest up.*

He is saying we should talk of it all the time, fathers, not just in one session. When they are at home, when they are out, when they go to bed and when they get up.

God knows that faith comes by hearing and the more they hear his word the deeper it roots into their spirits.

But we should be wise and not bug our children to death. God is not telling us to talk to them so much that we make them angry. He says in his word:

**Colossians 3:21**
*Fathers, provoke not your children to anger: lest they be discouraged.*

After you have had the initial chats with them, you can take advantage of things like television programs to continue to help them. It's easy to find a subtle example of illicit sex on TV. You can comment every now and then on the situation on the screen and how the word of God applies to it. This can teach them to be discerning television watchers.

### Your Son Wants You To Teach Him

When I was struggling with my wife's request that I teach my son, I decided to ask him if he wanted me to talk to him about sex. Maybe somewhere down deep I was hoping he would say something like, "No, Dad, not really." Then I would be off the hook!

But he didn't say 'no.' He said 'yes.' And not only did he say yes, I perceived that certain look of expectancy about it in his eyes. He seemed to have a thirst for me to talk with him. I knew for certain at that moment that there was no turning around.

My son not only wanted to be told about sex. He wanted the official version and he wanted it from me. And fathers, in the same way, I believe your children want it from you.

**Fathers Are Priests of Their House**

As spiritual leaders of our households, we are responsible to do as the scriptures say and:

> **Proverbs 22:6**
> *Train up a child in the way he should go: and when he is old, he will not depart from it.*

And also to:

> **Ephesians 6:4**
> *Bring them up in the nurture and admonition of the Lord.*

In this way, we will be worthy of the calling that God placed on Abraham, who was called the "Friend of God." The scriptures tell us that God picked Abraham to father his "chosen people" because he knew that Abraham would teach his children to keep the ways of the LORD:

> **Genesis 18:19**
> *For I know him, **that he will command his children** and his household after him, and they shall keep the way of the Lord...*

And as Abraham did what God told him, we must do what God tells us to do. We must command our children so they will not depart from the way of the Lord. It is not optional, it is a command.

**A Priest Who Blew It**

Now I am going to tell you about Eli. Eli was a priest in ancient Israel who blew his responsibility to teach his sons. In spite of the fact that they also were priests, his sons were worthless scoundrels and whoremongers.

They were so depraved that they committed two horrible sins. First, they took for themselves the offerings the people brought to the LORD and used them to satisfy their own lusts.

It got so bad that the people did not want to give offerings anymore. And the second thing they did was to misuse the women. They demanded and had sex with the women who came to the tabernacle. As the scriptures say:

**1 Samuel 2:17,22**
*17 Wherefore the sin of the young men was very great before the LORD: for men abhorred the offering of the LORD.*

*22 Now Eli was very old, and heard all that his sons did unto all Israel; and how* **they lay with the women** *that assembled at the door of the tabernacle of the congregation.*

As you would expect, God was not the least bit pleased with this, prophesying among other things the following about Eli:

**1 Samuel 2:29, 34, 36**
*29 ... and honourest thy sons above me, to make yourselves fat with the chiefest of all the offerings of Israel my people?*

*34 ... thy two sons, Hophni and Phinehas, in one day they shall die both of them.*

*36 And it shall come to pass, that every one that is left in thine house shall ... say, "Put me, I pray thee, into one of the priests' offices, that I may eat a piece of bread."*

And these prophecies came true in a big way. Eli fell and broke his neck when a messenger reported the death of his two sons. As it is written:

**1 Samuel 4:18**
*... that he fell from off the seat backward by the side of the gate, and his neck brake, and he died: For he was an old man, and heavy.*

**Help Your Son Get the Blessings**

Your son or daughter might ask questions like, "What's in it for me? Why should I do this? Are there any benefits?" Well I would like to share with you what God says about the benefits of keeping his word.

The real reason they should keep God's word is their love for Jesus. It was Jesus who said, "If a man love me, he will keep my words." (John 14:23) But young people, especially, need to know what the love of Jesus means in their lives.

As you will see, the benefits are not just going to heaven. God promises and delivers, **if** we keep his word. And the benefits are simple. He promises health, wealth, and heaven. But I don't want you to just take my word for it. I want to show you them in the scriptures.

A comprehensive listing of God's promises are in the 28th chapter of Deuteronomy. Throughout the travels of the Hebrew people in the forty years after they left Egypt, God revealed his will to them through signs and miracles confirmed by his word through Moses.

As the people were about to enter the Promised Land, Moses summarized the blessings of keeping God's words and the curses of not keeping His words.

The first 14 verses of the chapter contain the blessings. Following are the conditions for receiving the blessings:

> **Deuteronomy 28:1-2**
> ...*If thou shalt hearken **diligently** unto the voice of the LORD thy God, **to observe and to do** all his commandments ... that the LORD thy God will set thee high above all nations ... and **all these blessings** shall come on thee, and **overtake** thee, if thou shalt hearken unto the voice of the LORD thy God...*

Before I list the blessings I want you to notice the conditions — diligently, not just sometimes; to observe and to do, not just to observe. The blessings are automatic **if** the diligent observing and doing takes place.

Now let's take a look at a few of the blessings:

> **Deuteronomy 28:3-14**
> *Blessed shalt thou be:*
>
> *1. In the city (city life)*

2. *In the field (rural life)*
3. *Fruit of thy body (healthy babies)*
4. *Thy ground (good crops)*
5. *Thy kine (livestock)*
6. *Thy basket and thy store (food)*
7. *Coming in*
8. *Going out*
9. *Thine enemies ... shall come against thee one way and flee seven ways.*
10. *The **LORD shall command the blessing upon thee** in thy storehouses*
11. *Command the blessings upon thee in **all** thou settest thine hand unto*
12. *Make thee **plenteous in goods***
13. *Make thee the **head and not the tail***
14. *Thou shalt be **above only**, and thou shalt **not be beneath**...*

**if** *thou hearken unto the commandments of the LORD thy God, which I command thee this day...*

If this list didn't excite you, go back and read it again. It is simply awesome!

Unfortunately, the curse of the law is equally awesome, but very negative. It begins with, "But **if** thou wilt not hearken unto the voice of the LORD thy God, to observe to do..."

Suffice it to say, the cursings are opposite the blessings. Instead of "Blessed shalt thou be...", God says, "Cursed shalt thou be..."

But we who are partakers of the divine nature of Jesus Christ are redeemed from the curse of the law, Jesus Christ having been made a curse for us, as it is written:

**Galatians 3:13-14**
*13 **Christ hath redeemed us from the curse of the law**, being made a curse for us: for it is written, 'Cursed is every one that hangeth on a tree:'*

*14 **That the blessings of Abraham might come on the Gentiles through Jesus Christ;** that we might receive the promise of the Spirit through faith.*

Another scripture in the New Testament confirms that we are to be blessed and not cursed:

**3 John 1:2**
*Beloved, I wish above all things that **thou mayest prosper and be in health, even as thy soul prospereth.***

**Save Your Son from Destruction**

The twentieth century is not the only time that mankind has been destroyed because of sexual sin. Throughout the centuries God has dealt with sexual sinners beginning with the days before the Flood, through Sodom and Gomorrah, the ancient nation of Israel (Judah) all the way through today.

Just a brief review of some of the history of sexual sin and how God dealt with it:

**The Flood**
   **Genesis 6:5,7**
   *5 And God saw that the wickedness of man was great in the earth, and that every imagination of the thoughts of his heart was only evil continually.*

   *7 And the LORD said, I will destroy man whom I have created from the face of the earth.*

**Sodom & Gomorrah**
   **Genesis 18:20**
   *20 And the LORD said, "Because the cry of Sodom and Gomorrah is great, and because their sin is very grievous;*

   *21 I will go down now, and see whether they have done altogether according to the cry of it, which is come unto me; and if not, I will know:*

   **Genesis 19:13**
   *For we will destroy this place, because the cry of them is waxen great before the face of the LORD; and the LORD hath sent us to destroy it.*

### Jerusalem & Judah (Israel)
### Isaiah 3:8-9

*8 For Jerusalem is ruined, and Judah is fallen: because **their tongue and their doings** are against the LORD, to provoke the eyes of his glory.*

*9 The shew of their countenance doth witness against them; and they declare their sin as Sodom, they hide it not. Woe unto their soul! For they have rewarded evil unto themselves.*

What God is saying in this latter case is the homosexuals had come out of the closet and flaunted their sins just as the Sodomites before them had done. Their **tongues were doing things against the LORD.**

One of the worst times of sexual immorality was when priests actually allowed prostitutes to sell their bodies to men in the temple. Of this situation, God says through the prophet Hosea:

### Hosea 4:6

***My people are destroyed for lack of knowledge;*** *because thou hast rejected knowledge, I will also reject thee, that thou shalt be no priest to me: see thou has forgotten the law of thy God, I will also forget thy children.*

When we begin to teach our children what "thus saith the LORD," our society will not be "destroyed for a lack of knowledge." We will not be under the dreadful curse of the law.

That means we will have fewer and fewer children having children, unwed fathers or unwed mothers, adultery, homosexuality, lesbianism, suicides or bodies diseased with AIDS, syphilis, gonorrhea, genital herpes or the like.

Instead our sons and daughters will grow in health and prosperity as God wants them to grow. And we, having done our jobs, will hear the words, "Well done thou good and faithful servant."

## Chapter 3

## What & When to Teach Your Son

---

What should you teach and when should you teach it?

A son about to get married needs to know about sex in great detail. He is becoming the head of a family, a family that looks to him for leadership.

But small children about to enter nursery school needs to know something about sex too. They are becoming a part of a "world family", a family that may look to them for sexual molestation.

So what we teach them and when we teach them is driven by both their spiritual and biological needs as well as the influences they are subjected to in the society.

And since it is easier to teach them what God has to say about sex than to change their minds from what the 'world' has to say about sex, we need to teach them as early as possible.

But how did our society get to the point where grade schoolers need to know something about sex? What are the spiritual roots of this 'hobby' attitude toward sex?

This chapter shares my opinion of what children should be taught and when they should be taught it. In addition, it reviews some of the significant events that have lead to sexual immorality in our society and the spiritual roots of the forces underlying them.

It is my prayer that you and your family be blessed by the revelations contained herein.

**Four Year Old Kids Know**

A good friend of mine overheard a comment from a little girl she was babysitting that shocked her. One day the child blurted out, "They're kissing today, they're gonna go to bed tomorrow!" She was watching an afternoon soap opera on television.

What is this? She hadn't even been talking very long! But with just a year or so of watching soap operas, she not only knew about sex, she knew about the foreplay that precedes it!

What has happened to our society? If this child isn't taught something before she goes to elementary school, what will she learn there? Worse yet, what will she do there?

What it boils down to is this. Our sons and daughters are getting the world's message on sex — when to do it, how to do it, who to do it with.

If we don't teach them about sex early enough, the society at large will do it for us. But when the society does it, our children learn sin. When we do it using the word of God, our children learn holiness.

**Seduction of A Society**

But how did we get to this point when just some 50 years ago, people ran screaming out of movie theaters when they heard an actor say,
"Frankly my dear, I don't give a ----."

While ---- was a word that people may have used privately, they were outraged and shocked at the seemingly public endorsement of it on the "big screen." But that was only a beginning.

In the early fifties the seduction intensified, focusing on the minds of men. Exalting man above God, philosophers promoted the "power of positive thinking" saying things like, "Believe in yourself" rather than to "Believe in God." Also saying, "Have faith in your abilities" instead of saying to "Have faith in God."

Their teachings deceived many men to believe that they are their own judge, "knowing the difference between right and wrong." These philosophies are remarkably similar to Satan's deception of Eve in the Garden of Eden when he said, "Ye shall be as gods, knowing good and evil." And their teachings have resulted in suffering and humiliation not unlike that suffered by Adam and Eve.

And while the "big screen" of movie cinema had ushered lust into public places, the "small screen" of television was to bring lust into private places, the private places of our homes.

Although television initially balked at nasty and irreverent antics of various performers, they found their market share growing as a result of the lust.

In light of the dollars "at risk", they would not turn away from obvious sin. After all, when it came to the bottom line, money was their god. They felt compelled to compete for the advertising revenues that increased market share would bring.

And it didn't matter whether they were smut peddlers outright or just 'good' people trying to sell cosmetics, magazines, newspapers, coffee or beer. The centerfolds of yesteryear's girlie magazines were to become full page advertising in the most prominent newspapers and magazines. The seducing spirits of prior years had done their job.

"Frankly my dear, I don't give a ----," had become so mild that movies with lines like that are shown to almost any audience. The hard stuff these days start with nudity, goes on to include vaginal penetration, excretion and bestiality. And this is not just on the big screen, but on small screens in our homes.

**Sexmania Society**

Today the continued application of progressively more vile pornography has seared people's ability to discern the difference between what is holy and what is sin. People are leaving the things of God, as it is written:

**1 Timothy 4:2**
*Giving heed to seducing spirits, and doctrines of devils; Speaking lies in hypocrisy; having their conscience seared with a hot iron.*

The generations of 50 years ago, long since being titillated by the 'good' taste of the forbidden fruits, are watching their children of today suffer. As it is written:

**Ezekiel 18:2**
*The fathers have eaten sour grapes, and the children's teeth are set on edge.*

That taste of yesterday's fruit has exploded into the teeth of AIDS, children having children, child molestation, teenage suicide, unwed mothers, and unwed fathers.

But despite this, the society-at-large looks for solutions with condoms, school sex clinics and abortions. They have come to love pleasure more than they love God.

And some do these things giving lip service to God, having a form of godliness, but denying the power thereof. As it is written:

**2 Timothy 3:2-7** *(excerpts)*
*For men shall be lovers of their own selves... disobedient to parents... unholy... without natural affection ... **lovers of pleasures more than lovers of God**; Having a form of godliness, but denying the power thereof... Ever learning, and never able to come to the knowledge of truth.*

## "Faith" for Sin Comes By Hearing Satan

And just as faith in the things of God comes by hearing, and hearing by the word of God, so does faith in the things of Satan come by hearing. But the hearing is by the word of Satan!

So as the society has heard and heard and heard the words of Satan, they are believing and acting on them. Satan, using the mouths of humanistic philosophers and men trying "be all **they** can be" deceive the people saying, "Keep on sinning, but use condoms."

And the worst part of it is Satan has also deceived some of the people called by God's name, his very elect. They say the same thing with a slight variation, "Don't sin, but if you do, 'use condoms.'"

One of the worst things about the seduction of our society is the disguises Satan uses when he does it. He does not come in a red suit with a pitch fork. Instead, he comes as philosophers espousing the power of man himself.

They even mock the failure of man when he fails trying to be all he can be, saying its wonderful when man hits bottom because when he's on the bottom there's no place to go but up.

I don't know what is so wonderful about hitting bottom. I'm sure your son or daughter would much rather be "the head and not the tail" and "above only", and "not beneath" as God promises us in Deuteronomy 28:13.

Besides, Jesus hit bottom for us when he died and came back up as the scripture says:

> **Ephesians 4:10**
> *He that descended is the same also that ascended up far above all heavens, that he might fill all things.*

And there is another place that you can go besides up. Just ask any victim of AIDS —those who have AIDS or those who live in fear of AIDS.

Or ask any parent of an unwed teenage mother or father. Or ask a drug addict who can't live with drugs ... and can't live without them.

Or you can ask someone who tried to 'be all he could be' only to find himself dumped and forgotten after he was burned out by his institution.

Or you can ask the parents of a teenager who, out of a feeling of failure, dropped out of life committing suicide. Or ask a street person who may have never even had hope.

Or you can ask someone whose heart is ravaged with disease or whose stomach is full of ulcers or someone who has high blood pressure.

Or you could ask the neglected children, the battered wives, neglected husbands or the mental institutions.

Yes, there is somewhere to go besides up. You can die. And you can die in misery without living the victorious life that God wants you to live.

**Philosophers Round off the Word**

What the philosophers have really done is to round off the word of God, deceitfully leaving out the name of Jesus and exalting man. For example, while the scripture says:

> **Philippians 4:13**
> *I can do all things **through Christ** which strengthens me.*

the philosophers get our young people to think only of the first part, "I can do all things." They cunningly leave Jesus out of the picture. The thing Satan accomplishes with these nice sounding phrases is thievery. He steals the word of God from your children as he stole it from me as a child (See Chapter 1).

And when Satan succeeds in stealing the word of God, just as he stole it from Eve in the Garden, he proceeds to kill and destroy people with the sin they fall into.

When we have the word of God first and foremost in our spirits, Satan can not penetrate us. The following scripture from Ephesians puts it well, calling the word of God "armour:"

> **Ephesians 6:11**
> *Put on the whole armour of God, that ye may be able to stand against the wiles of the devil.*

When the word of God is stolen, even because someone has made us believe we can 'be all we can be', we are easy prey.

And we parents have fallen into the same trap. We have extended the power of positive thinking to direct our children to do things like the following:

- Be an independent thinker.
- Just make something out of your self.
- Be somebody.
- Make a name for yourself.
- Be the best you can be.
- Just get an education—you'll have it made.

And the sin is this. We have left God out of the picture. And if we have included God at all we have invoked his name as a byword. And when God is left out, we are in trouble.

## "Faith" for Holiness Comes By Hearing God

So what all of this means then is that we fathers must teach our sons and daughters "with the word of God" from the earliest possible age. They must hear it day and night to counteract the epidemic proportions of sexmania and humanistic philosophies.

I know you have heard of the "generation gap." Your parents probably said there was a generation gap between you and them. And you probably see a gap between you and your children.

But the generation gap is a gap only to the Godly values of past generations. On the other hand the un-Godly decadence of my father's day and his fathers day has rushed across a "Generation Bridge" gathering with it the sludge of worsening sexual sins.

We have witnessed a gap to the good, but a bridge to the bad.

## A Model Time Line For Teaching Your Children

With this as a sketchy portrait of the society we live in today, I am offering a model for what and when you should teach your children. This model is just that. A model. It is my opinion of the most appropriate school year to teach your children the facts of life.

Clearly however, you should observe your children to know when they are hearing words that can soften them up for sin. If they are hearing the wrong message from any source, you need to counteract it with the word of God immediately, even if they are as young as four years old. It much easier to teach a fertile mind than to teach a contaminated mind.

**Talking Pre-Schoolers**

Your sons and daughters need to grow up with the name of Jesus grafted in their hearts. They should sing it when they wake up, in the middle of the day and when they go to bed at night. Jesus is the power that rejects spirits like those trying to seduce the four year old my friend baby sat.

They should be taught that their spirits and souls will live forever. And when and if someone close to you or them dies, let the child know that their spirit and soul still live.

This spiritual truth is a foundation stone to not only their sexual morality, but their overall outlook on life. You see, if they believe the lie that when life's over it's over, they will satisfy the flesh. As the word says:

> **1 Corinthians 15:32**
> *...If the dead rise not? Let us eat and drink; for to-morrow we die.*

But when they know, without question, that they have eternal life with God or eternal damnation with Satan, it makes a difference in they way they behave.

As part of this teaching I suggest you not teach them the prayer that says:

> Now I lay me down to sleep. I pray the Lord my soul to keep. If I should die before I wake, I pray the Lord my soul to take.

That prayer is a prayer of doubt, not a prayer of faith. There should be no question as to where their soul goes at death. Have your children thank God for their eternal life through Christ Jesus when they pray.

**When They Go to Nursery or Elementary School**

Now this is where the influences really start to come to your children. You have covered them in your nest with your feathers all their lives. But now they are going into the world. So what do you tell them?

I suggest you tell them about the three types of love mentioned in Sex Lesson No. 1. They already knows about the Agape love of God. After all, you have had them singing "Jesus loves me, yes I know..."

They should also knows about Phileo love, having experienced the friendship of their parents and perhaps even a brother, sister, cousin or neighbor friend.

So now all you have to do is tell them about that special love that is only meant for a man and his wife. That is the special love that produced them in their mother's body.

You could use words like the following. I will call your son "Billy" just for this example:

Dad: You know that Jesus loves you, Billy?

Billy: Yes, Daddy.

Dad: You also know that your mother and I love you, too?

Billy: Yes, Daddy.

Dad: Do you know that we loved you before you were born?

Billy: I don't know what you mean, Daddy.

Dad: What that means is that your mother and I wanted you to be born so we loved each other with a special kind of love to plant you in your mom's body.

Billy: Do you mean sex, Dad?

Dad: Yes. Sex is a special kind of love that God only wants a man and his wife to have.

Billy: But I've seen people look like they are doing that on television, and they aren't married to each other.

Dad: I know son, but that is because of evil in people. Even if they were married, sexual love should be done in private.

Billy: Oh!

Dad: So what I want to tell you Billy is this: Sexual love is only for man and wife. Any other sex is sin.

Billy: Oh!

Dad: So if anyone tries to touch you and molest you like those people you hear about on the television news, tell them to "Stop in the name of Jesus." Then tell me or your mom right away. We love you as Jesus loves you. The people who do that kind of thing are sick and we need to pray for them.

If Billy should say something like, "Tell me more about sex Dad, how you and mom do it." Let him know that you will teach more about it when he is older.

**Entering Jr High School**

Sometimes between the beginning of junior high school and entering high school you should teach your children about sex. The basic message is simple. Sex is meant only for people married to each other. All other sexual practices are sin.

Your children should be taught to obey the will of God, only knowing that certain perverted sexual practices exist, but not having expert knowledge of them. As the scriptures say:

> **Romans 16:19**
> *For your **obedience** is come abroad unto all men. I am glad therefore on your behalf: but yet I would have you **wise unto that which is good**, and **simple concerning evil**."*

In addition, they need to know which sexual practices are sin even within a marriage relationship. And they should know all of this from scripture, not from any worldly wisdom you may have. My son told me that he wouldn't have accepted what I told him if I didn't back it up with God's word.

**Drug & Other Works of the Flesh**

Drug abuse is a sin. As you will see in the last lesson on sex, drugs are a form of witchcraft and, as such, are sin. This should be taught at least by the time your children enter junior high school.

If you even suspect drug use in their environment before this time, educate them on God's word in this area. In addition, you should cover the spiritual aspects of Sex Lesson No. 1 before discussing the drug issue.

## When He is About to Get Married

Your son is on the way to getting married when he first meets his wife. And vice versa. And this can happen as early as 15 years old! Because of this, I strongly recommend you teach your children the lessons on marriage as soon as they start to 'go steady.'

You may have to screen certain portions of them depending on how close they actually are to marriage. Most importantly, by doing so early, they can avoid being unequally yoked with unbelievers.

In addition, before the relationships with these 'would be' spouses get too close, your son or daughter will know the scriptures to apply in determining whether or not the other person is acceptable.

## Teach Them All The Time

Children are not necessarily forgetful. If they were, they would forget both the bad and the good, not just the good. What really happens to them and us is this: Someone steals the good words from them. As it is written:

> **Mark 4:14-15**
> *14 The sower soweth the word.*
>
> *15 And these are they by the way side, where the word is sown; but when they have heard, Satan cometh immediately, and taketh away the word that was sown in their hearts.*

And the reason Satan steals the word is so he can kill and destroy them. As it is written:

> **John 10:10**
> *The thief (Satan) cometh not , but for to steal, and to kill, and to destroy...*

Since he is trying to steal the word, you will want to review these lessons according to the following scripture:

> **Deuteronomy 6:7**
> *...and shalt talk of them when thou sittest in thine house, and when thou **walkest by the way** and when thou **liest down**, and when thou **risest up.***

At a minimum, I would suggest a formal review of the Lesson Overviews with your child at least once a year, if not more.

## Chapter 4

# Why the Name of Jesus Overcomes

The power is in the name of Jesus.

Your son or daughter can win their battles against sexual sin if they observe and use the word of God. This may, on occasion, require them, to utter words like:

"In the name of Jesus, NO!" Or:
"In the name of Jesus, STOP!" Or:
"In the name of Jesus, OUT."

In doing so however, they must know in the depths of their hearts who Jesus is and why at the name of Jesus every knee must bow and every tongue confess that Jesus Christ is Lord to the glory of God (Philippians 2:10-11). It must be real to them. It must not just be a popular statement or a buzzword.

### The Power of Positive Thinking is Limited

Our sons and daughters must not be left with only their own "self will" or "will power" to abstain from sexual sin. Just like our generation, they are not strong enough. If all we teach them can be summarized in words like these, they are bound to fail.

"Just say, NO."
"Just don't do it."
"You can abstain if you say you can."
"You can do anything you try to do."
"You've got the will power."

The reason they will fail is this: Even if they succeed in the flesh, they will fail in their hearts. You see, even the fantasies of their heart are sin too. As Jesus said:

**Matthew 5:28**
*But I say unto you, "That whosoever looketh on a woman to lust after her hath committed adultery with her already in his heart."*

By even trying to live by "self will", they would be denying Jesus Christ and the power of the Word of God in their lives. The word of God does say, "I can do all things", but it includes two key words to go along with them. "I can do all things **through Christ**". It's the "through Christ" part where the power of God is invoked.

In addition, by living according to self will, they would be subjecting themselves to the substitution rule of the world which says: "You've got to have at least one vice, if you don't smoke, drink. If you don't drink, do drugs." Besides, your children should live their lives with great joy and power, not with sadness or feeling they are in prison to a set of rules.

As you teach them using the word of God, they will have that joy and power. And knowing that the battles in their life are spiritual, and not physical, they will know that the power of positive thinking needs Jesus Christ to be lasting in their lives.

**The Spiritual Genetic Code**

To illustrate the power in the name of Jesus, I am sharing in this chapter how the spiritual aspects of man's genetic codes are evidenced in the scriptures. I trust it will be a blessing to you as you prepare to teach your children.

And while the revelations herein may tend to strengthen one's faith in God, I caution the reader not to run off and try to understand

God from it. It is merely one of countless revelations that the word of God has about life.

**The Genes in the Flesh**

Man has known about heredity since virtually the beginning. He had only to look at his sons and daughters to know that heredity existed. But it has only been in this, the twentieth century, that man discovered how such characteristics are carried in the body. Scientists say they are evident in the genes. Thus another science was born — the science of genetics.

**Genetic Engineering**

Not only does science know about genes and their impact on man, they also know how to alter them through what is called "genetic engineering' and 'gene splicing'.

They are researching the genes for clues to a multitude of diseases including the dreaded AIDS. They report seeing 'secret codes' in our bodies and actually refer to them as if they were a real alphabet.

They say they see these codes in the blood, the marrow and the semen, even in some cases tying genes to cancer and to certain abnormal behaviors. Newspaper headlines, in fact, say things like:

> GENES MAY PLAY ROLE IN CONTRACTING AIDS
>
> Research Indicates Abnormal Gene May Cause Elephant Man's Disease.
>
> DECIPHERING THE BLOOD'S SECRET CODE
>
> Researchers Race to Find Clues to Immunity
>
> BREAST CANCER MAY BE TIED TO RARE GENE
>
> RESEARCHERS MAY HAVE FOUND GENETIC CLUE TO SCHIZOPHRENIA

**What Does Genetics Prove?**

While early research into genes was done to prove the 'theory of evolution,' what did their research really prove? Clearly man did not evolve from apes as researchers wanted to show; the Book of Genesis makes that clear. And who wrote the code? Any scientist, especially a computer scientist knows that codes have to be written.

And who designed the system? Science also knows that code generally goes into a system after that system has been designed and built, in this case the human system. And who contaminated the codes with deformed physical genes, the genes of sickness and disease, the genes of insane behavior patterns—the genes that kill and destroy man. These questions are not answered by science.

**The Genes of the Spirit**

But the good news is that the word of God does answer these questions. And not only does the word answer them, it also tells us that the original genetic code in man was not only good, it was "very good." It also tells us how man himself is the gatekeeper, opening his doors for more contaminated coding to come into his body and mind.

More importantly, however, the word of God tells us the means of escape. It tells us how to overcome the powers that both write and operate on the defective codes. And it tells us that Jesus, the writer (author) of the original code, came back to reclaim man as man's kinsman redeemer, his best friend. As the scripture says:

> **Hebrews 12:2**
> *Looking unto Jesus the **author and finisher** of our faith; who for the joy that was set before him endured the cross, despising the shame, and is set down at the right hand of the throne of God.*

**The Invisible Things...**

Being spiritually blinded to 'be all he can be', man gets so caught up developing and proving theories of life that he doesn't know that he, himself, is evidence of life. He tries to find proof through the laboratory when the word of God is the real proof.

Not only that, as the virtually **invisible coding of the genes** are seen though the microscope, they are also evidence. And not just evidence of God, the contaminated coding is also evidence of Satan. As the scriptures say about the invisible things of God:

**Romans 1:20**
*For **the invisible things** of him from the creation of the world are clearly seen, being understood by the things that are made, even his eternal power and Godhead.*

To help you see how the scriptures bear out the invisible things of God in man and the contamination of man by Satan, I have summarized these revelations before discussing them in greater detail. They are presented from the standpoint of the scriptures themselves.

1. God created man with a genetic coding that was "very good." Man was to live forever.

2. Adam's sin allowed Satan to contaminate man's genetic coding, naming our code "Satan", giving us his Law of Sin and Death.

3. God so loved man that he promised to put his laws into our inward parts, to **write** them (the code) in our hearts, and to give us power over Satan.

4. Jesus Christ and the indwelling Holy Spirit are the "first step" in fulfillment of that promise, our code being renamed "Jesus", giving us his Spirit of Life.

5. As our sons and daughters hear and act on the word of God, they are in the "continuous second step" of rewriting their code.

6. God's Spirit of Life and Satan's Law of Sin and Death co-exist in the Christian, man still being able to choose either holiness or sin.

7. As our sons and daughters utter the words of God in the name of Jesus, they invoke the power of God to overcome the powers of Satan.

8. At the Rapture of the Church, Jesus will call those who have his name in their genetic coding.

9. The Millennium will see man live hundreds of years again as Satan will not be able to act on the spiritual genetic coding of the Law of Sin and Death.

### 1. God Made Man with A Very Good Genetic Coding

**Genesis 2:7**
*And the Lord God formed man of the dust of the ground, and breathed into his nostrils the **breath of life**; and man became a living soul.*

(It should be noted that the Hebrew word translated breath means spirit.)

And we know that there were no genetic defects in Adam's genetic code. After all, the scriptures say it was not only good, "it was very good." Man was to live forever.

**Genesis 1:31**
*And God saw every thing that he had made, and behold, **it was very good.***

### 2. Sin Gave Satan Dominion Over Man

The word of God says to whom you obey, that is your master. As it is written:

**Romans 6:16**
*Know ye not, that to whom ye yield yourselves servants to obey, **his servants ye are to whom ye obey**; whether of sin unto death, or of obedience unto righteousness?*

So when Adam sinned, he became Satan's servant. And Satan thereby put **his** name (Satan) on man, thereby altering man's genetic coding. This was the origin of death as well as sickness and disease.

So why did Satan come? Jesus answers that question in John 10:10 speaking of Satan as the "thief":

**John 10:10**
*The thief cometh not, but for **to steal**, and **to kill**, and **to destroy**: I am come that they might have life, and that they might have it more abundantly.*

The first thing Satan stole was the word of God. He knew that Eve would fall without it. So by getting her to doubt the word of God, he stole it. Then he was able to kill and destroy Eve; and thru her, Adam.

And he does the same thing today. First he doesn't want your children to get the word of God. But if they get it, he tries to steal it so he can kill and destroy them.

It is as if Satan has tapped into our umbilical cord to God, imposing his nature on us, working death and deterioration in our bodies and minds through destructive coding of the genes. As the scriptures say:

**Romans 6:12**
*Wherefore, as by one man (Adam) sin entered into the world, and death by sin; and so death passed upon all men, for that all have sinned.*

And it is perfectly clear that the current epidemic and scare of AIDS is an outgrowth of sin. Homosexuality is sin. Fornication is sin. Adultery is sin. And sin allows Satan to write more of his code of sickness and death into man. Satan gets his authority through the sin. That's why Romans 6:23 says, "The wages of sin is death..."

God's spirit strove with man at least until the Flood when God became grieved by man's wickedness. As it is written:

**Genesis 6:5, 3**
*5 And God saw that the wickedness of man was great in the earth, and that every imagination of the thoughts of his heart was only evil continually.*

*3 And the LORD said,* **"My spirit shall not always strive with man,** *for that he also is flesh; yet his days shall be an hundred and twenty years.*

The accelerated degeneration of man since the Flood is clear when we see from scripture that Adam and the men born before the Flood lived from almost 800 years to slightly less than 1000 years before they died. This is in marked contrast to man of today where a man in his nineties is considered old.

And whereas Adam fathered Seth at 130 years old and Noah fathered Shem at 500 years old, it is rare for 70 year old men to father children today.

Not withstanding the ability of their flesh, the first men had tremendous brain power as well. Adam named all of the animals without the aid of a computer, having the use of all of his brain. This is in contrast to today when, science tells us that twentieth century man uses less than one per cent of his brains.

### 3. God Promised to Redeem Man and Give Him Power

God knew when he cursed the Serpent in the Garden of Eden that he was going to send Jesus to redeem his people (Redeem means to buy back). When he cursed him he said:

> **Genesis 3:15**
> *And I will put enmity between thee and the woman, and between thy seed and* **her seed***; it shall bruise thy head, and thou shalt bruise his heel.*

So when Jesus came some 4000 or so years later as **the seed of Mary**, he was fulfilling that prophecy.

But God continued to prophesy at many times in between, especially when He prophesied through the prophet Jeremiah some 600 years before Mary that he would "write" his laws into man's heart.

This writing was into man's genetic coding. As it is written:

> **Jeremiah 31:33**
> *After those days saith the Lord, I will put my law in their* **inward** *parts, and* **write** *it in their hearts; and will be their God, and they shall be my people.*

God prophesied through the prophet Joel some 800 years before Jesus that he would give us the Holy Spirit:

> **Joel 3:28, 32** (excerpts)
> *28 And it shall come to pass afterward,* **that I will pour out my spirit on all flesh\*;** *and your sons and your daughters shall prophesy, your old men shall dream dreams, your young men shall see visions:*
>
> *32 And it shall come to pass, that* **whosoever shall call on the name of the LORD shall be delivered.**

\* 'all flesh' means Gentiles in addition to Jews. Between the Flood and Jesus, the Holy Spirit only resided with people for a period of time to achieve God's will in specific purposes.

## 4. Jesus and the Indwelling Holy Spirit Fulfill the Promise

When God puts his law in man's **inward parts**, that constitutes the new birth that Jesus told Nicodemus about when he said:

> **John 3:3**
> *Verily, verily, I say unto thee, "Unless a man be born again, he cannot see the kingdom of God."*

("Verily, verily" means this is really important, I want you to listen closely.)

It represents a kind of spiritual transfusion of the blood of Jesus into our bodies, a transformation in which our genetic coding is given a new name, the name of "Jesus." We receive a transfusion from our spiritual Father.

As Jesus said:

> **John 6:54**
> *...Verily, verily, I say unto you, Except, ye eat the flesh of the Son of man, and drink his blood, ye have no life in you.*

> **Luke 22:20**
> *Likewise also the cup after supper, saying, "This cup is the new testament in my blood, which is shed for you."*

This rebirth, through the shed blood of Jesus, is similar to the birth of a natural baby. As a woman's "water breaks" before childbirth, Jesus passed both water and blood at the cross as it is written:

> **John 19:34**
> *But one of the soldiers with a spear pierced his side, and forth with came there out **blood and water**.*

And the power through the Holy Spirit is confirmed by many scriptures including Jesus before he ascended into heaven. As it is written:

> **Luke 24:49**
> *And, behold, **I send the promise of my Father upon you**; but tarry ye in the city of Jerusalem, until ye be endued with power from on high.*

And also in the book of Acts where it is written:

> **Acts 1:8**
> *But ye shall receive power, after that the Holy Ghost is come upon you.*

## 5. The Code is Re-Written Through Faith

In one act, a public confession out of his heart that Jesus Christ is the Son of God and that God raised him from the dead, man receives Jesus and becomes a spiritual babe in the Lord.

But, after any baby is born it must be fed, first with the milk, but graduating to the meat as the baby grows into adulthood — in this case, adulthood in Christ.

God's law is written into that man's heart **in a continuous process as he hears the word of God.** He must hear the word of God as it is written:

> **Romans 10:17**
> *So then faith cometh by hearing and hearing by the word of God.*

> **Hebrews 11:6**
> *But without faith it is impossible to please Him; for he that cometh to God must believe that He is, and that He is a rewarder of them that diligently seek Him.*

Having faith can be described as knowing and acting on the word of God. If man doesn't have the word of God, he can't have faith. If he doesn't have faith, he can't please God. It's impossible.

## 6. The Spiritual Genetic Codes Co-exist

The Christian man still has the Law of Sin and Death in him despite his acceptance of Jesus Christ. Operating spiritually, much like the law of gravity works physically, this law makes a man want to obey his flesh no matter what his mind wants to do. Even

Paul, the penman of the Book of Romans, speaks of this force inside of him, calling it a law. As it is written:

**Romans 7:21-23**
*21 I find then a law, that, when I would do good, evil is present with me.*

*22 For I delight in the law of God after the inward man:*

*23 But I see another law in my members, warring against the law of my mind, and bringing me into captivity to the law of sin which is in my members.*

So fathers, as this great man of God had a war in his members trying to make him sin, truly your son or daughter has the same war in their members. And this war is in addition to the peer pressures working on them from the outside.

But our God is permissive. He does not force man to accept Jesus Christ. Neither, once a man has accepted Jesus, does he force him to accept all the benefits thereof such as healing or prosperity.

Nor does he make him **not sin**. Man remains a free moral agent, free to choose good or evil. He is not condemned to die if he walks after the spirit. As it is written:

**Romans 8:1-2**
*1 There is therefore now **no condemnation** to them which are in Christ Jesus, who walk not after the flesh, but after the Spirit.*

*2 For the law of the Spirit of life in Christ Jesus hath made me free from the law of sin and death.*

But if the Christian man should sin wilfully (walking after the flesh), mocking Jesus by trampling on his blood, thinking that God will have to forgive him, it is written:

**Hebrews 10:26, 30**
*26 For if we sin wilfully after that we have received the knowledge of the truth, **there remains no more sacrifice for sins**.*

*30 For we know him that hath said, "Vengeance belongeth unto me, **I will recompense**," saith the Lord.*

That man has walked away from the sacrifice of Jesus Christ. God says he will repay that man.

As the non-Christian man sins, that's what can be expected of him. He is under the Law of Sin and Death. At the very root of his being, his intents are sinful. It is in his heart. He has the sinful nature that Satan gave Adam. And he does the Works of the Flesh, no matter how 'good' they may appear on the surface.

**7. The Name of Jesus Invokes the Power**

With the teachings in this book, your son or daughter will know that the battles in their life are not physical, but spiritual. As it is written:

> **Ephesians 6:12**
> *For **we wrestle not against flesh and blood**, but against principalities, against powers, against the rulers of the darkness of this world, against spiritual wickedness in high places.*

They will know how to exercise the (dominion) power that Adam didn't exercise over Satan. They will do as Jesus said in Luke:

> **Luke 10:19**
> *Behold, I give unto you power **to tread on serpents and scorpions**, and **over all the power of the enemy**: and nothing shall by any means hurt you.*

The **serpents** are the spiritual forces like the Serpent that deceived Eve. **The power of the enemy** is the power of Satan and his demonic host to operate on the Law of Sin and Death in man's members — in his genetic coding. And also as Jesus said in Mark 16:17

> **Mark 16:17**
> *And these signs shall follow them that believe; **in my name shall they cast out devils**; they shall speak with new tongues.*

When they know this, your sons and daughters will be able to do exactly what Jesus said they would be able to do. When the Holy Spirit witnesses to them, they will be able to say:

"In the name of Jesus, NO!" Or:
"In the name of Jesus, STOP!" Or:
"In the name of Jesus, OUT!"

And they will get the results too. Their tempters will get weak in the knees. Although they may ridicule them, swear at them or mock them, they will flee. No power can stand up to the name of Jesus properly used by a Christian.

Your son or daughter will also know the value and importance of getting rooted and grounded in the word of God. In that way, they can be more than conquerors in life, not just in overcoming sexual sin, but also in becoming the victorious person God wants them to be. As it is written:

**Romans 8:37**
*Nay, in all these things we are **more than conquerors through him that loved us.***

An example of the name of Jesus overcoming disease was when Peter and John saw a man who had been born lame lying at the gate to the temple. As it is written:

**Acts 3:6-9**
*6 Then Peter said, "Silver and gold have I none; but such as I have give I thee: **In the name of Jesus Christ** of Nazareth rise up and walk.*

*7 And he took him by the right hand, and lifted him up: and immediately his feet and ankle bones received strength.*

*8 And he leaping up stood, and walked, and entered with them into the temple, walking, and leaping and praising God.*

### 8. Jesus Will Call Those With His Name

At his second coming, commonly called the Rapture, Jesus will call all men who have his name in their spiritual genetic code and who are looking for him at his coming. As it is written:

**Hebrews 9:28**
*So Christ was once offered to bear the sins of many; and **unto them that look for him** shall he appear the second time without sin unto salvation.*

Somewhat analogous to the way you can call your bank account through an automatic teller or the way a computer programmer calls a program by its name, Jesus will call all Christians, both those who are alive and the bodies of those who have died. They still have his name in their spiritual coding. As it is written:

**1 Thessalonians 4:16-17**
*16 For the Lord himself shall descend from heaven with a shout, with the voice of the arch angel, and with the trump of God: and the dead in Christ shall rise first:*

*17 Then we which are alive and remain shall be caught up [raptured] together with them in the clouds to meet the Lord in the air; and so shall we ever be with the Lord.*

And fret not. Much like "bar-coded" food products in a grocery store, every hair on our head is coded, so Jesus will call all of us. We will be "checked out" from the physical to the spiritual (It should be noted that law enforcement scientists are able to identify rapists from a scientific examination of the (dead) pubic hairs they leave on their victims.) As it is written:

**Luke 12:7**
*But even the very hairs of your head are all numbered. Fear not therefore.*

### 9. Long Life Returns During the Millennium

After the seven year Tribulation period ending with the battle of Armageddon, the Law of Sin and Death will remain in man, but Satan will not be around to operate on it. He will be bound for a thousand year period that is called the Millennium. As it is written:

**Revelations 20:2**
*2 And he laid hold on the dragon, that old serpent, which is the Devil, and Satan, and bound him a thousand years.*

Man's life expectancy and his genetic coding will return to that of the men before the Flood. Their childhood will last a hundred years, as it is written:

> **Isaiah 65:20**
> *There shall be no more thence an infant of days, nor an old man that hath not filled his days: for the child shall die an hundred years old...*

### "Self Will" Is Not Acceptable to God

So as the most well meaning Christian tries to please God through his "self will" or the "power of positive thinking", without the word of God, he simply can't do it.

It is only when he knows the word of God that he can act on it whether he's acting to raise his moral behavior, to bring about healing in his body or to bring about prosperity in his life.

Jesus, himself, recognized this "self will" in man early in his ministry when many believed after they saw the many miracles he did. The scriptures tell us:

> **John 2:24-25**
> *25 And needed not that any should testify of man:* **for he knew what was in man.**

Jesus could spiritually discern the Law of Sin and Death working in man. He could see it in their genes.

### Judas Failed Because of "Self Will"

The scriptures further testify to two important aspects of the power of the word of God over the Law of Sin and Death. First it shows that man can be clean through the word. But second, it shows that even if the word is in man, man can still turn against God, if such is his will. Jesus said the following about the cleanness of his disciples:

> **John 13:10-11**
> *10 Jesus saith to him, "He that is washed needeth not save to wash his feet, but is clean every whit:* **and ye are clean, but not all.**
>
> *11 For he knew who should betray him; therefore said he,* **"Ye are not all clean."**

But later, after Judas Iscariot had left the room to betray him, Jesus told them they were clean, without making any exception, saying:

**John 15:3**
*Now ye are clean through the word which I have spoken unto you.*

Judas had a strong "self will" and desire for earthly power. He was disappointed after Jesus did not seize what he thought was an excellent opportunity to form an army to overthrow the hated Romans. This was after Jesus had miraculously fed the 5000 from five barley loaves and two small fishes.

Judas wanted to battle for a kingdom in the flesh. Jesus was winning the battle in the spirit. He served Jesus for the wrong reason. And he failed. As it is written:

**John 6:15**
*When Jesus therefore perceived* **that they would come and take him by force, to make him a king,** *he departed again into a mountain himself alone.*

**Teaching Your Children**

So in teaching your son or daughter the lessons in this book, they will be more than conquerors in overcoming sexual sin as they will know about life at its most fundamental level. Their vulnerability to sexual sin will be minimized as they know how to wage spiritual warfare.

And the best part of it is they can then abstain from sexual sin with great joy, not depression or anxiety, Jesus giving them both the peace and the power they want in their lives. They should not be overcome by the lust of their flesh, the lust of their eyes or the pride of their lives. They will know what the scripture means when it says:

**Acts 17:28**
*For in him [Jesus] we live, and move, and have our being...*

And being "in Him", they will be able to exercise the power he spoke of when he said:

**Matthew 28:18**
*...All power is give unto me in heaven and in earth.*

## Is Spiritual Genetic Code New?

I cannot close this chapter without telling you that the spiritual aspect of the genetic code is not new. It is just a twentieth century revelation of what God said in his word 2000 years ago.

Then he used an example of grafting a branch into a tree to explain how man can be grafted back into his Spirit. Rather than calling it 'genetic engineering' or 'gene splicing', he called it the 'root and fatness of the olive tree'. As it is written:

> **Romans 11:17**
> *And if some of the branches be broken off, and thou, being a wild olive tree, wert graffed in among them, and with them partakest of the root and fatness of the olive tree.*

Even in the days of Moses some 3,500 years ago, God said that children would suffer for the sins of their fathers if they hate him. But he said he would show mercy (healing) to those that love him and keep his commandments. Exodus 20:5-6.

## If This Makes Sense...

If the spiritual aspect of the genetic code makes sense, you are blessed. However, I want to caution you about trying to understand these words through your senses alone. That's because God's word is true whether we understand it or not.

For example, the senses of a first century man would probably have said that genetics, along with electricity, television, telephones, airplanes, space exploration and computers don't make sense. But that would not change the reality of their existence today.

In fact, men of that day, even the learned ones, had trouble understanding spiritual things from earthly examples. A classic example is when Jesus described the salvation of man by saying man must be "born again." As it is written, Nicodemus did not understand:

> **John 3:9**
> *Nicodemus answered and said unto him,*
> *"How can these things be?"*

**John 3:10, 12**
*10 Jesus answered and said unto him, "Art thou a master of Israel, and knowest not these things?*

*12 If I have told you earthly things, and ye believe not, how shall ye believe, if I tell you of heavenly things?*

If you were to try and understand it through your brain power you would be trusting in a facility that, scientists say, uses only one-one thousandth of its capability. This limited use of our brain power is a worldly reason we should look at caution toward those teachers of positive thinking who say we should "Do the best you can with what you've got." We would not be using very much.

When we exercise our faith in God, however, our minds are moved up until we have the mind of Christ. As it is written:

**Romans 12:2**
*And be not conformed to this world: but **be ye transformed by the renewing of your mind**, that ye may prove what is that good, and acceptable, and perfect, will of God.*

**1 Corinthians 2:16**
*For who hath known the mind of the Lord, that he may instruct him? **But we have the mind of Christ.***

So rather than trusting in themselves, your children should be taught to "observe and do" what the Maker of our brains tells us to "observe and do" in his word. This includes the well known scripture that says:

**Proverbs 3:5**
*5 Trust in the LORD with all thine heart: and lean not to thy own understanding.*

Through the prophet Isaiah, God demonstrates the futility of trying to understand the world we live in based only on what our senses tell us. Then God, some 2000 years before Columbus discovered America, tells us the earth is round and that we are like grasshoppers in his sight:

**Isaiah 40:22**
*22 It is he that sitteth upon the **circle of the earth**, and the inhabitants thereof are as grasshoppers; that stretcheth out the heavens as a curtain, and spreadeth them out as a tent to dwell in.*

So as you teach your sons and daughters, acting as a vessel for the gospel of Jesus Christ, there is no question in my mind that you will be successful. You will be teaching them how a just man lives. As it is written:

**Romans 1:17**
*The just shall live by faith.*

And what is faith?

**Hebrews 11:1**
*Now faith is the substance of things hoped for, the evidence of things not seen.*

It is important to note that this scripture does not say, "Now **sense** is...", Now **logic** is...", Now **education** is...", Now **understanding** is...", Now **science** is...", it says "Now **faith** is... Faith is living by the word of God.

And the word of God ensures your success. For God says in the Book of Isaiah:

**Isaiah 55:11**
*So shall my word be that goeth forth out of my mouth: it shall not return unto me void, but it shall accomplish that which I please, and it shall prosper in the thing whereto I sent it.*

His word, through you, will accomplish the purpose for which it was sent. It will not return unto him void.

## The Results

And when you have taught your children, they will know what to do when they are tempted. They will know when to ignore them, when to use the Word on them, and when to use the Name of Jesus on them.

And when they say, in the Name of Jesus, "NO", "STOP", or "OUT", they will know it is not them, but the Lord Jesus in them actually doing the work. As is written:

### John 14:13

And whatsoever ye shall ask [command] in my name, **that will I do**, that the Father may be glorified in the Son.

And when their tempters flee, there will be absolutely no question in their minds that . . .

The power is in the name of Jesus.

# Chapter 5

# *If You're Not Sure You're Saved...*

---

If you are not saved...or if you are not sure, you are showing the faith to receive salvation by reading this far in this book.

To reward that faith, Jesus will receive you right now, if you believe in Him and make the following confession.

I suggest you read it to yourself first. If you agree with it, then say it aloud to your new Father in heaven. You will be leaving the kingdom of darkness presided over by Satan and entering the Kingdom of Light presided over by God himself:

Dear Heavenly Father

I come to you in the name of Jesus

Your Word says, "Whosoever shall call upon the name of the Lord shall be saved" (Romans 10:13)

Your Word also says "if thou shalt confess with thy mouth the Lord Jesus, and shalt believe in thine heart that God hath raised him from the dead, thou shalt be saved. For with the heart man believeth unto righteousness; and with the mouth confession is made unto salvation." (Romans 10:9-10)

I believe in my heart that Jesus Christ is the Son of God. I believe that God raised Him from the dead for my justification. And I confess Him now as my Lord.

I have now become the righteousness of God in Christ (2 Corinthians 5:21).

I am redeemed from the curse of sickness, poverty and the second death (Galatians 3:13).

I was a sinner. Now I am saved by grace.

Thank you, Lord!

Welcome to the body of Christ. You have just been born again. The name of Jesus is now in your spiritual genetic code (Reference to Chapter 4). You are a "new creature" in Christ Jesus (2 Corinthians 5:17).

**What To Do After The Confession**

But as I also discussed in Chapter 4, you are now a spiritual babe in the Lord and must begin the continuous process of spiritual growth. I would suggest you do three things to ensure that growth:

1. **Find a bible believing, teaching and practicing church and join it.** (If you don't find a church you want to join right away, make your confession at some church anyway. Jesus wants you to confess him publicly. It helps build your faith.)

2. **Find and listen to Christian radio and television teaching programs.** These ministries can supplement the teachings of your church, but they should not continue to be your primary source of spiritual food.

   After you find a church that feeds you spiritually, your tithes should then go to that church, with only free will offerings going to radio and television ministries.

3. **If your children are not Christian, use the teachings you have received in these chapters to lead them to Jesus.** Your faith in God will be a strong testimony to them.

## Areas of Caution

Now that I've told you what to do, let me give you some things to look for and guard against as you do them.

### 1. Be Careful How You Hear

Be careful how you hear. Everything you hear in a church or on Christian radio or television is not scripturally Christian. As the scriptures say:

**1 John 4:1**
*Beloved, believe not every spirit, but try the spirits whether they are of God: because many false prophets are gone out into the world.*

The false prophets may talk about a "god" but not Jesus Christ. They cannot consistently say, with joy, that Jesus is Lord...that he was in the beginning...that he lived in the flesh...that he died...that he was resurrected...and that he ascended into heaven...that he will come again.

### 2. Teachings Against the Bible

First Century Christians in Berea, a city in what is now Greece, did not believe everything they were told. The tried the spirits by checking them against the scriptures (most likely Isaiah). You should do the same. As it is written:

**Acts 17:11**
*...[The Bereans] received the word with all readiness of mind, and **searched the scriptures daily**, whether those things were so.*

### 3. Seek The Church of Brotherly Love

A Bible teaching church is a church which both teaches **and** practices the scriptures line by line and precept by precept, from every part of the Bible. It does not concentrate on just one area of truth in the word of God.

The church of brotherly love teaches on salvation as well as prosperity, healing, morality, tithing and the like from both the Old and New Testaments. It practices the scripture which says:

**Isaiah 28:9**

*9 Whom shall he teach knowledge? And whom shall he make to understand doctrine? Them that are weaned from the milk, and drawn from the breasts.*

*10 For precept must be upon precept, precept upon precept; line upon line, line upon line; here a little, and there a little.*

### 4. The Church of Philadelphia Brotherly Love

When you find the church of brotherly love, you will have found a Church of "Philadelphia" as described in Revelation 4:7-13.

While Philadelphia was an actual congregation in Asia in the First Century, Jesus also uses it as representative of the ideal church. He has only the best of things to say about this church and did not say anything negative about them.

This is in contrast to two other general types of churches that exist today, namely the church of Laodicea and the church of Thyatira.

### 5. The Church of Laodicea Lukewarm Church

Jesus speaks to the church of Laodicea in Revelation 3:14-22.

This type of church is neither hot nor cold. And because it is lukewarm, Jesus will spue it out of his mouth. He is also knocking on the spiritual door of these churches so he can enter and sup with **any** man who hears his voice and opens the door.

If you find yourself in this type of church, listen for the knock and let him in to sup with you. He may lead you to find a Church of Philadelphia in your community.

### 6. The Church of Thyatira False Gods

Jesus speaks to the church of Thyatira in Revelation 2:18-29.

While Jesus knows the works, charity, service, faith, and patience of these churches, he chastises them about the spiritual fornication they are committing with Jezebel, the prophetess.

"Jezebel" is a figurative way of describing the worship of idol gods.

If you find yourself in this type of Church, I suggest you leave it and find a Church of Philadelphia in your community.

## 7. Salvation is Voluntary

Remember that salvation is only for whosoever will, not for whomsoever is made. If your children don't accept Jesus initially, don't force them. Rather, pray in the name of Jesus for God to draw them to Him.

Once again, welcome to the body of Christ. You have taken the first steps toward repenting from your sin. And as you grow in the word of God you will continue to repent as the Holy Spirit convicts (not condemns) you. Congratulations! This is the most important day in your life.

## Chapter 6

## How to Use This Book

This book is called Father to Son because I am a father and I taught my son. Its lessons are written in such a way, however, that they can be used for either married or single fathers or mothers for either their sons or daughters.

In addition, persons with ministry callings, special skills and special problems may also find the book useful.

**If You Are The Married Father of a Son...**

You should be ready to teach him after reading this book. I suggest your wife be very much aware of these lessons as well. That way, she can reinforce the scriptures when appropriate.

**If You Are The Married Parents of a Daughter...**

Both of you should share in teaching your daughter. I would suggest the father take the lead in teaching the spiritual parts with the mother/wife handling those portions of lessons that refer to sexual intercourse.

**If You Are A Single Father of a Daughter...**

You should teach her the spiritual lessons. However, I would suggest you have some "aged woman" (Titus 2:1-6) assist you in teaching those portions of lessons that refer to sexual intercourse.

**If You Are A Single Father of a Son...**

You should be ready to teach your son after reading this book.

**If You Are A Single Mother of a Daughter...**

You should be ready to teach your daughter after reading this book.

**If You Are A Single Mother of a Son...**

You should teach him all of the spiritual lessons. However, I would suggest you have some "aged man" (Titus 2:1-6) assist you in teaching those portions of lessons that refer to sexual intercourse.

**If Your Son or Daughter Have Left Home...**

Without being taught about sex and marriage, I suggest you send them a copy of this book. They will always be your children even if they are heads of their own houses.

**If You Are A Child or Teenager...**

Your parents or guardian should teach you. However, if they are not available to do the teaching, I suggest the following:

Second choice is to have a close relative (uncle, aunt, grandparent, etc.) who meets the requirements of an "aged" man or woman listed in Titus 2:2.

Third choice is to have a teacher provided by a "Philadelphia" type church". (Such a church will not turn you down.)

Fourth choice is to teach yourself. (If you do this, be sure to read the scriptures aloud.)

**If You Are An Evangelist...**

You may be able to use this book as both an evangelistic outreach and as a teaching tool, especially in ministries involving families, young people, students, home study, prisons and etc.

## If You Are A Pastor...

Your sheep know your voice and they will be looking to hear these teachings from you. If they don't, some may leave to receive at other congregations.

I suggest therefore, that at the leading of the Holy Spirit, you do the following:

1. Use it as source material for sermons on the subjects of sexual morality and marital fulfillment.

2. Teach the sex and marriage lessons as part of your Sunday School and Bible Studies.

3. Teach the marriage lessons especially, as part of marriage encounter-type teaching vacations.

4. Train a select group of "aged men" and "aged women" to teach or assist in teaching children about sex and marriage.

5. Make this book available for resale to the general public from your church.

6. Participate with other churches in community wide campaigns to teach parents how to teach their children.

(Write the author c/o the Publisher for information on how to order books, Teacher Guides and/or establish community-wide campaigns.)

## If You Set Church Educational Policy...

I would suggest a policy wherein all parents in your church be taught how to teach their children about sex and marriage according to the following schedule:

**Teaching about sex...**
Parents will be taught how to teach their children about sex before they enter junior high school.

**Teachings about sex & marriage...**
Parents will be taught how to teach their children about both sex and marriage before they graduate from high school.

**If You Are A Broadcaster...**

You can support area churches in community-wide teaching campaigns by actively promoting them over your programs, radio and television stations.

**If You Retail Books...**

You can help stem the tide of sexual immorality by aggressively offering this book to everyone who enters your store. Don't just put it on shelf.

Keep a supply at your counter for this purpose.

**If Your Marriage is Separated...**

Or strained toward separation, you can use the word of God to heal it, no matter how bad the problems.

As you and your spouse willingly use these words, you will be reconciled to each other just as God used Jesus as the word of God to reconcile the world to himself. As it is written:

> **2 Corinthians 5:19**
> *19 ...that God was in Christ, reconciling the world unto himself, not imputing their trespasses unto them; and hath committed unto us the word of reconciliation.*

And just as God does not impute (charge) us with our trespasses neither should we impute our spouses with theirs.

**If You Have AIDS...**

You need to know that the name of Jesus is higher than the name of AIDS. And as a Christian you can be healed, even if you have AIDS as a result of sexual sin or drug addiction.

But you must repent and turn to God. A "Philadelphia" type church can help you. They know that it is not by their might or power, but by God's Spirit that healing comes about. (See Chapter 5 for a description of this type of church.)

Once healed however, you must grow in the word of God and not go back to sin. If you do, something seven times worse than AIDS will come upon you. As Jesus said to a man he had just healed:

**John 5:14**
*...Behold, thou art made whole: Sin no more, lest a worse thing come unto thee.*

And if you have AIDS as a result of someone else's sin, you must forgive. For if you forgive not, your healing may be hindered.

## Chapter 7

## How to Teach the Lessons

I taught my son after searching the scriptures for those applying to sex and marriage. Since they are reprinted in this book, you will not have to do the same research.

However, I strongly recommend you use a structured approach such as the one outlined in this chapter. It is in keeping with the scripture which says:

**1 Corinthians 14:40**
*Let all things be done decently and in order.*

**General Teaching Guidelines**

I also recommend you follow the general teaching guidelines I have listed following:

1. Read every word of this book **before** teaching your son or daughter.
2. Review this chapter on "How to Teach the Lessons" before **each** teaching session.
3. Pray for the success of **each** teaching session, in agreement with and in the presence of your son or daughter.

4. Make an appointment for **each** session.

5. Teach in a private place and at a time acceptable to both of you.

6. Teach only as long as you have their attention. If you teach longer, your efforts may be in vain.

7. Allow enough time between lessons to let the words sink in, but it is suggested you go no longer than a week between lessons.

8. Review the Lesson Overviews with them at least once a year thereafter.

**Suggestions For Using The Bible and This Book**

Father to Son is designed to be used with the Bible. I suggest it be used as your guide during the teaching along with a Bible, preferably the King James Version.

1. If possible, please provide your son or daughter with a Bible they can use while you are teaching.

2. If they are unfamiliar with the Bible, find the Bible page numbers in advance for each scripture you will be reading and write it on the teaching pages of the lessons.

3. Provide them a list of the scriptures you will be using before, or after each teaching session as you prefer. (You may reproduce the list provided at the end of each lesson.)

4. You should read the scriptures to them ALOUD. It can also be helpful to let them re-read some scriptures back to you.

5. Write notes in the book to remind you of additional things you may want to say as you teach. Space is provided.

6. Autograph and give this book to your child when he or she gets married and leaves home. It can be used in their marriage and for teaching their children.

**Pray for the success of the teaching**

The first thing to do before starting the teaching is to pray for its success. I strongly recommend you pray for the following at the start of each teaching in the presence of your son or daughter:

Dear Father God, I pray:

1. That you will anoint my heart and my lips to teach your word with the love of Jesus.
2. That you will circumcise my son's ears that he may hear, and his heart that he might receive the teachings.
3. That you will give us favor with each other in this teaching.
4. That you will receive all the glory and honor from the teachings.
5. That no forces in or outside of this place will, in any way, hinder the teachings.
6. I thank you for answering this prayer.
7. I give you the praise and the honor for the words you have given me.

In the Name of Jesus, I pray. AMEN.

**Making An Appointment**

There is a lot of value in making an appointment. These discussions are far too important to spring on anybody without any notice. It can be done as simply as this:

> Son, you are growing up and I think it's time for the two of us to sit down and talk about the facts of life. Why don't we do it on (date/time)?

Set a time and place convenient for the two of you. This builds up their expectations and gives them time to get ready for the chat.

**Answering the Tough Questions**

There is a chance that some sons, especially, may respond with some tough questions when approached about sex. With all of the situation comedies on television, they are certainly being groomed to catch you by surprise. This is how I would suggest certain tough responses be handled:

### If Your Son Says He Isn't Ready...

And just in case your son says he isn't ready to hear all that kind of stuff, don't breath a sigh of relief! Make an appointment with him anyway, at least for the first lesson. Let him know that it is laying a spiritual foundation for his growth.

It can also make it much easier to give him the second lesson when he is ready. And he could be ready in as soon as a few weeks to a few months. Kids grow up fast.

### If Your Son Says He Knows Everything...

If your son says he "knows all that stuff", just let him know you want him to know what God says about the facts of life. And even if he has heard what God says about it, make an appointment anyway.

This gives you a chance to make sure of what he knows and to drive the principles deeper into his spirit. More importantly, you will be taking your rightful position as his counselor and guide.

### If He Says He'll Tell You Whatever You Want To Know...

If your son says something like, "I'll tell you whatever you want to know, Dad," don't panic! Don't get caught up in the trap that maybe he has heard of some sexual technique or perversion that you haven't heard of before.

Besides, your teaching is about the spiritual aspects of the facts of life more so than body functions. You are teaching him God's word on sexual morality.

Make an appointment anyway. Tell him that you are going to tell him what God has to say about sex. But when you do have the chat, keep the communication channels open. Let him talk. If he is interested in sexual perversions, the word of God that you teach him will drive it far from him.

### If Your Son Has Been Involved In Sexual Sin...

If your son has been involved in sexual sin, and either he tells you or you have reason to believe that he is, it is extremely important that you make an appointment with him. He needs the word of God in the worst way.

Don't be angry at him. Neither should you be proud of him "being a chip off the old block" or anything like that. In making the appointment let him know that you want to talk to him about what God says about sex.

**Answering the Tough Questions About Your Past...**

If your son were to ask you a question like:

> Dad, were you as good as you are telling me to be? Did you have sex with mom or anyone else before you got married?

Whether you did or didn't is not important. If you did, maybe your son could say, "Well how can you tell me anything righteous?" or if you didn't, your son could say, "How can you tell me anything worthwhile!" I would suggest this answer:

> "Son, my life has not been perfect. No one taught me what I'm going to teach you. [Only of course if it's true.] I'm just glad that I have confessed my sins and been forgiven. And since God says he won't remember them anymore, I don't plan to remember them either."

(The following scripture covers confession and forgiveness.)

**1 John 1:9**
*If we confess our sins, he is faithful and just to forgive us our sins, and to cleanse us from all unrighteousness.*

(The next scripture tells us that God chooses not to remember our sins.)

**Hebrews 10:17**
*And their sins and iniquities will I remember no more.*

**Picking the Place to Talk**

The place you teach is important. To teach in a place where you normally discipline could be a disaster. Make sure it is reasonably private. No one else should be able to overhear what you are talking about.

A poor place could distract not only you but your son or daughter as well. I say this because your home is not the only place you can teach.

My son and I talked about some parts of it in a fast food restaurant. The timing was right and no one else was within earshot. One night we talked about it in the TV room and another time in his bedroom as he was about to go to bed. He liked the TV room the best.

**Go No Longer Than His Attention Span**

There is something about my son's eyes that tell me he's had enough. And if I miss that signal and go much longer his body language starts to say the same thing. And if I keep going, treating him as a computer that can absorb and digest everything in one conversation, he starts to tell me in words that he has had enough. Being a respectful son, he knows within his mind the scriptures that say:

> **Exodus 20:12**
> *Honor thy father and thy mother: that thy days may be long upon the land which the Lord thy God giveth thee.*

But as I continue to talk beyond his attention span, I find myself about to provoke him, if not to anger, to perhaps frustration. As the scripture says:

> **Colossians 3:21**
> *Fathers, provoke not your children to anger, lest thy be discouraged.*

But you know your children. You know their attention span. And your job is to make sure you don't go beyond it. When you see signs of fatigue or saturation, stop. You can resume the lesson another time. Overkill can do just what it says, kill everything you have gone over.

**Time Between Teaching Lessons**

I am recommending you teach your son or daughter in several lessons. By splitting it up, they will have an opportunity to digest the scriptures and be prepared for subsequent lessons.

But you should not hold yourself to one session per lesson if your child's attention span is shorter than the time it takes to cover the material. Any lesson may be split in half if need be. The important thing is to cover all of the material in a way that it goes into your child's spirit.

The time between lessons also provides you an opportunity to chat with your son or daughter about sex on an informal basis. Especially if they are uptight during the scheduled teaching session, this gives you time to cover some key points when they may be more receptive.

Time between lessons also gives you a chance to reinforce the teaching by, for example, showing how certain television programs deceive people into thinking sexual sin is harmless.

**Power of the Words of God**

As a father, you will know whatever opportunities are open to you and I urge you to seize them. Just remember to stay 'at rest' accepting the fact that you are merely the vessel and that the word of God is doing the work. As the scripture says:

**Hebrews 4:12**
*For the word of God is quick, and powerful, and sharper than any two edged sword, piercing even to the dividing asunder of soul and spirit, and of the joints and marrow, and is a discerner of the thoughts and intents of the heart.*

**2 Timothy 3:16**
*All scripture is given by inspiration of God, and is profitable (good) for doctrine, for reproof, for correction, for instruction in righteousness:*

**Shared Reading of Scriptures**

Your son or daughter can share in reading the scriptures. But one thing is very important in light of the following scripture.

**Romans 10:17**
*So then faith cometh by hearing, and hearing by the word of God.*

So they must hear it. It must come through their "ear gates" as such. And your voice, the voice of authority in their life should be the vessel to say it. I suggest you be sure and read every scripture to them.

## Using Bibles When You Talk

Although this book includes the scriptures you will be reading, I recommend very strongly that you have your Bible with you during the teaching. This reinforces the fact that you are the vessel that God is using to deliver his word, not the source.

As such you are not coming on as a pillar of virtue who has not been touched by the sins of this world, it is God speaking through you. The following suggestions could be very helpful:

> First, get your son or daughter a Bible if they don't already have one. It is important for them to be able to re-read, in private, the scriptures you teach them.
>
> Second, note in this book the page numbers from his (or her) Bible of the scriptures you will be reading. This is really helpful if they are not familiar with the Bible.

If a second Bible isn't available, don't let that get in the way. Teach them anyway. Let them use any Bible for their private reading.

## Do Not Teach The Details of Sexual Sin

In keeping with the scriptures, you should only teach your children that certain kinds of perverted practices exist but not make them experts on them.

Neither should you make them experts on condoms, contraceptives, so called 'safe sex', venereal diseases or the like. The world is full of that kind of stuff. But God wants us to avoid such teachings. He says this in the following scriptures:

> **Romans 16:17**
> *Now I beseech you, brethren, mark them which cause divisions and offences contrary to the doctrine which ye have learned; and avoid them.*

Not to fight the people who want to teach such things, but to know who they are and to avoid them.

And the scriptures go on to say that these people, who may use reasonable arguments ("good words and fair speeches"), don't serve God, they serve mammon:

**Romans 16:18-19**

*18 For they that are such serve not our Lord Jesus Christ, but their own belly: and by **good words** and **fair speeches** deceive the hearts of the simple.*

*19 For your obedience is come abroad unto all men. I am glad therefore on your behalf: but yet I would have you **wise unto that which is good and simple concerning evil.***

Being "wise unto that which is good" means knowing and doing God's word. Being "simple concerning evil" meaning just knowing that certain evils exist, but to avoid them.

Another scripture which says the same thing in a different way is as follows:

**Romans 12:9**
*...Abhor that which is evil; cleave to that which is good.*

Therefore, if your child should ask about any details of sexual sins, these scriptures can be your response.

**Teaching the Lessons**

Teaching should be customized to a method you are comfortable with AND a method which gets the scriptures into your child's spirit.

The lessons are divided into two parts. The first part is an overview which you should read to your child. The second part is detailed teaching pages which provide chapter and verse for each of the major points of the overview.

a. *The column on the left hand side of the page is the actual scripture from the Bible. This is what you should read initially. They are printed in a style like this paragraph.*

b. The column on the right hand side of the page has comments and remarks that you can make as you teach each scripture.

(In some cases, definitions are provided for words. The words in parenthesis are intended to guide you and not necessarily to be read to your child.)

c. As you get to each new point, be sure to ask if he or she has any questions.

**Notes In the Book**

As you read this book, especially the lessons, I suggest you make written notes directly in the book as necessary. They can be extremely helpful when you do the actual teaching. Space is provided for this in several places.

**Give the Book to Your Son**

When your son or daughter gets married, I suggest you autograph this book and give it to them, suggesting they teach their children from the same book.

In addition, the Closing Comments following Pre-Marriage Lesson No. 7 can be very helpful in focusing their marriage toward success.

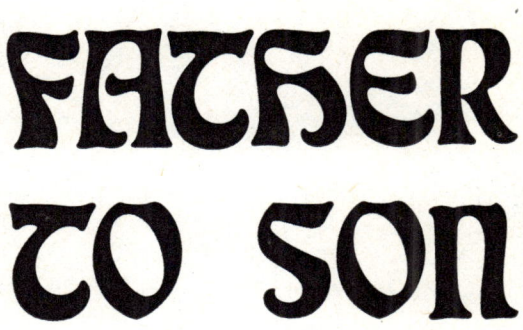

# FATHER TO SON

Volume II

Lessons
On
Sex

*Overview*
*Sex Lesson No. 1*

# Your Spiritual Foundation In Jesus

---

The next time we get together I will be teaching you about sex. But today I will be teaching you about some spiritual things you need to understand before we talk about sex.

    I You are spirit, soul and body.

   II Your spirit and soul will live forever.

  III Your eternal life is with Jesus Christ.

  IV Your body is the Temple of the Holy Spirit.

    V Only one type of love is sexual.

  VI Treat girls like your sister

 VII Love requires obedience

VIII I will teach you how to love your wife.

*Sex Lesson #1*

## I. You Are Spirit Soul and Body

The soul has the mind, ego and senses.

**Hebrews 4:12**
*For the word of God is quick, and powerful, and sharper than any two edged sword, piercing even to the dividing asunder of **soul** and **spirit**, and of the joints and **marrow**, and is a discerner of the thoughts and intents of the heart.*

"Marrow" represents the body.

**2 Corinthians 4:16**
*For which cause we faint not; but though our **outward man** perish, yet the **inward man** is renewed day by day.*

'Outward man' is the body.
'Inward man' is the spirit.

**1 Peter 3:4**
*But let it be **the hidden man of the heart,** in that which is not corruptible...*

The 'hidden man of the heart' is the spirit.

**1 Thessalonians 5:23**
*And the very God of peace sanctify you wholly; and I pray God your whole **spirit** and **soul** and **body** be preserved blameless unto the coming of our Lord Jesus Christ.*

God says it precisely. Man is spirit, soul and body.

**Notes:**

**Genesis 1:27**
*So God created man **in his own image** created he him; male and female created he them.*

We are made in God's image so we are what God is.

**John 4:24**
*God is a Spirit: and they that worship him must worship him in spirit and in truth.*

Since God is a Spirit, we are spirits.

I can conclude this by saying: You are a spirit. You have a soul and you live inside of a body.

## II Your Spirit and Soul Will Live Forever

**1 Corinthians 15:22-23**
*22 For as in Adam all die, even so **in Christ** shall all be **made alive.***

*23 But every man in his own order: **Christ the first fruits;** afterward they that are **Christ's at his coming.***

You will get a new body in the Resurrection.
Jesus was resurrected first. Our bodies will be resurrected when he comes back.

**2 Corinthians 5:8**
*We are confident, I say, and willing rather to be **absent from the body,** and to be **present with the Lord.***

When we die physically, our spirits and souls leave the body and go to Christ in heaven.

**1 Corinthians 15:43-44**
*43 It is sown in **dishonour;** it is raised in **glory:** it is sown in **weakness;** it is raised in **power;***

Sex Lesson #1

*44 It is sown a **natural body;** it is raised a **spiritual body.** There is a natural body, and there is a spiritual body.*

Our bodies will resurrect from corrupt, dishonored, weak and natural bodies. We will receive incorrupt, glorious, powerful and spiritual new bodies.

### III Your Eternal Life is With Jesus Christ

**1 Corinthians 15:51-52**
*51 Behold, I shew you a mystery;* **We shall not all sleep,** *but we shall all be changed,*

*52 In a moment,* **in the twinkling of an eye,** *at the last trump: for the trumpet shall sound, and* **the dead shall be raised incorruptible,** *and* **we shall be changed.**

What this means is if Jesus comes back before our bodies die, we will be raptured (caught up) with him in the heavens.

Special Note:
This is not inconsistent with science since they say: "Matter cannot be created or destroyed, it only changes its form." We merely go from the physical to the spiritual.

**Notes:**
_____
_____
_____
_____
_____
_____

## IV Your Body Is the Temple of the Holy Spirit

The next thing you should know is that when you accepted Jesus Christ as your personal saviour your body became the temple of God's Holy Spirit.

**1 Corinthians 6:17-20**
*17 What? Know ye not that he which is joined to an harlot is one body? For two, saith he, shall be one flesh. But **he that is joined unto the Lord is one spirit.***

*18 Flee fornication! Every sin that a man doeth is without the body; but **he that committeth fornication sinneth against his own body.***

Your body is the temple of the Holy Ghost (Spirit). God's Spirit lives inside of you.

*19 What? Know ye not that **your body is the temple of the Holy Ghost** which is in you, which ye have of God, and ye are not your own?*

It is mocking God for Christians to commit sexual sins.

*20 For **ye are bought with a price:** therefore glorify God in your body, and in your spirit, which are God's.*

The price was Jesus. His bloody crucifixion, death, burial and resurrection.

**Special Comment:**
Since your body is the temple of God's Holy Spirit. If you commit a sexual sin, you are disgracing God's temple. It is as if you committed a sexual sin at the pulpit of a church.

*Sex Lesson #1*

## V There Are Several Types of Love—Only One is Sexual

In the English language we use the word L-O-V-E to express several slightly different attitudes toward someone or something.

You can generally tell which love is meant by how it is used.

If you will read a few scriptures I will tell you what the Greek word was for love.

**John 3:16**
*For God so **loved** the world, that he gave his only begotten Son, that whosoever believeth in him should not perish, but have everlasting life.*

**Matthew 5:44**
*But I say unto you, **Love** your enemies, bless them that curse you...*

**Mark 12:38**
*And he said unto them in his doctrine, "Beware of the scribes, which **love** to go in long clothing, and **love** salutations in the marketplaces.*

**1 Peter 3:8**
*Finally, be ye all of one mind, having compassion one of another, **love** as brethren, be pitiful, be courteous.*

**Agapao.** This is the love of God. It is unconditionally given to everyone. (He loved us before we became Christians)

**Etheleo.** This is the love where someone delights in something.

**Philadelphos.** This is the love of a brother. Like brotherly love.

**Titus 2:4**
*That they may teach the young women to be sober, to **love** their husbands, to **love** their children.*

There are a whole string of Greek words that start with **p-h-i-l.**

This comes from their root word **phileo** meaning friend.

Two different Greek words are used for love in this scripture.

**Philoteknos** for love to the children.

**Philandros** for love to the husband.

### VI  Treat Girls Like a Sister

**1 Timothy 5:2**
*Intreat ... the elder women as mothers; the younger as sisters, with all purity.*

**Special Comment:**
**Philandros,** the love for a husband is the only type of love that should include sexual affection. (Another Greek word for sexual love is **eros** or **erotic**).

In God's order of things it is meant only for the man and woman within the marriage institution.

Simply put:
- Agapao love is for all.
- Phileo love is for the close ones.
- Erotic love is for the marriage.

*Sex Lesson #1*

## VII  Love Requires Obedience

The fundamental definition of love is in the scriptures:

**1 John 4:8**
*He that loveth not knoweth not God; for **God is love.***

God is Love

**John 14:23**
*If a man love me, he will keep my words; and my Father will love him, and we will come unto him, and make our abode with him.*

Love of God requires obedience.

**John 14:24**
*He that loveth me not keepeth not my sayings: and the word which ye hear is not mine, but the Father's which sent me.*

If a man doesn't love God, he won't keep his words.

**Special Comment:**
As you can tell from this, if you are to please God you must keep his words. And to keep his words you must know his words.

## VIII  I Will Teach You How to Love Your Wife

Either I or some aged man should teach you how to love your wife sexually.

Also, some aged woman should teach your wife how to love you.

**Titus 2:1-6**

*1 But speak thou the things which become sound doctrine:*

*2 That the **aged men** be sober, grave, temperate, sound in faith, in charity, in patience.*

*3 The **aged women likewise,** that they be in behaviour as becometh holiness, not false accusers, not given to much wine, teachers of good things;*

*4 That they may **teach the young women** to be sober, **to love their husbands,** to love their children,*

*5 To be discreet, chaste, keepers at home, obedient to their own husbands, that the word of God be not blasphemed.*

*6 **Young men likewise exhort** to be sober minded.*

This love is **philandros** including **erotic** love.

If your father doesn't teach you, an **aged** man **with the qualities listed** should teach you.

(A man without those qualities and a younger man could be motivated by such teaching to go after your wife for himself. Or a homosexual after you.)

Your wife should also be taught by an aged woman with the **qualities** listed.

(A woman without those qualities or a younger woman could be motivated by such teaching to go after the husband for herself. Or a lesbian after your wife.)

*Sex Lesson #1*

## Scriptural References for Sex Lesson No. 1
### (This list may be reproduced for your son or daughter.)

**You are spirit, soul and body.**
Heb 4:12 of soul and spirit, and of the joints and marrow
2 Cor 4:16 outward man perish, yet the inward man is renewed...
1 Pet 3:4 But let it be the hidden man of the heart, in that...
1 Thes 5:23 your whole spirit and soul and body be preserved...
Gen 1:27 God created man in his own image created he him...
Jn 4:24 God is a Spirit

**Your spirit and soul will live forever.**
1 Cor 15:22-23 in Christ shall all be made alive...at his coming.
2 Cor 5:8 to be absent from the body...present with the Lord.
1 Cor 15:43 sown in dishonour...glory, sown in weakness...power...
1 Cor 15:44 sown a natural body, raised a spiritual body...

**Your eternal life is with Jesus Christ.**
1 Cor 15:51 we shall not all sleep, but we shall all be changed..
1 Cor 15:52 in the twinkling of an eye...we shall be changed.

**Your body is the temple of the Holy Spirit.**
1 Cor 6:17 he that is joined unto the Lord is one spirit.
1 Cor 6:18 flee fornication...committeth fornication sinneth...
1 Cor 6:19 your body is the temple of the Holy Ghost...
1 Cor 6:20 ye are bought with a price, therefore glorify God...

**There are several types of love—only one is sexual**
Jn 3:16 For God so loved the world, that he gave his only...
Mt 5:44 But I say unto you, Love your enemies, bless them...
Mk 12:38 which love to go in long clothing and love salutations..
1 Pet 3:8 love as brethren, be pitiful, be courteous.
Tit 2:4 to love their husbands, to love their children...

**Treat girls like a sister.**
1 Tim 5:2 Intreat...the younger as sisters, with all purity..

**Love requires obedience**
1 Jn 4:8 He that loveth not knoweth not God: for God is love.
Jn 14:23 If a man love me, he will keep my words...
Jn 14:24 He that loveth me not keepeth not my sayings...

**I will teach you to love your wife.**
Tit 2:1 speak thou the things which become sound doctrine.
Tit 2:2 be sober, grave, temperate...faith...charity...patience.
Tit 2:3 likewise...holiness..not false accusers..not..much wine.
Tit 2:4 teach the young women to....love their husbands...
Tit 2:5 to be obedient to their own husbands...
Tit 2:6 Young men likewise exhort....

*Overview*
*Sex Lesson No. 2*

# The Basic Facts of Life

The last time we got together we talked about Your Spiritual Foundation of your life. Today we are going to talk about the basic facts of life where it comes to sex. We will be talking about:

    I  What sexual intercourse is

    II  That sexual intercourse is ONLY for people married to each other.

    III  How babies are made

    IV  How girls and boys are changing

    V  The significance of virginity

    VI  That certain kinds of sex are sin even between people married to each other, including:

        A  Adultery

        B  Fornication

        C  Prostitution

        D  Masturbation

*Sex Lesson #2*

    E  Oral Sex — Anal Sex

    F  Homosexuality — Lesbianism

    G  Incest

    H  Sex with Mother & Her Daughter

    J  Bestiality — Sex with Animals

VII  Abortion is sin.

VIII  Abortion is sacrifice to idol gods

## I What is sexual intercourse?

Sexual intercourse is the union between a man and a woman when the man's erect penis enters a woman's vagina.

They are stimulated during this act leading up to an orgasm when the man ejaculates semen into her vagina.

**Notes:**

*The Basic Facts of Life*

## II What & Who Is Sexual Intercourse For?

Sexual intercourse is for:

• Procreating the human race through a husband and wife.

**Genesis 4:1**
*And Adam knew Eve his wife; and she conceived, and bare Cain, and said, I have gotten a man from the LORD.*

• Pleasure between a man and his wife.

She "conceived" means she got pregnant. It takes about 9 months for the baby to come.

**Proverbs 5:18**
*Let thy fountain be blessed: and rejoice with the wife of thy youth.*

"Fountain" refers to his sex organ.

## III How Are Babies Made?

When the man's sperm (in his semen) fertilizes a woman's egg a baby is conceived.

A woman's menstrual is when she bleeds from her vagina once a month for 3 to 5 days.

When she is pregnant, she stops menstruating as the blood starts to feed the baby. A fully developed baby comes out through the vagina.

Sex Lesson #2

## IV How Your Body is Changing

Girls start to menstruate at age 10 to 15.

They start to develop breasts about the same time.

The breasts are to feed babies milk.

Boys and girls start to get sexual urges.

Both boys and girls start to grow hair in their pubic areas and under their arms.

Boys begin to develop hair on their faces too.

## V Is Virginity Important To Marriage    Yes!

**Hebrews 9:18-20**
*18 Whereupon neither the first testament was dedicated without blood.*

*19 For when Moses had spoken every precept to all the people according to the law, he took the blood of calves and of goats, with water, and scarlet wool, and hyssop, and sprinkled both the book, and all the people.*

Blood is important in the establishment of permanent covenant relationships.

A virgin has a membrane over her vagina. It is broken by her husband's penis as he enters her on their wedding night. That blood flowing over his penis is symbolic of the permanent covenant their marriage becomes.

*20 Saying, "This is the blood of the testament which God hath enjoined unto you."*

*Mark 14:24 And he said unto them. "This is my blood of the new testament, which is shed for many."*

*Genesis 2:24 Therefore shall a man leave his father and his mother, and shall cleave unto his wife: and they shall be* **one flesh.**

These scriptures show two blood covenants in the Bible. First when God renewed a blood covenant through Moses. (Covenant and testament mean the same thing.)

A second covenant is the blood covenant Jesus cut with anyone who will believe in him.

He considers his covenant with us as permanent.

(The Old Testament laws regarding a virgin wife are in Deuteronomy 22:13-29.

When this blood is shed in the wedding night bed, a man and his wife become **one flesh.**

## VI Different Kinds of Sexual Sins

### A Is Adultery Sin — Yes

Adultery is sexual intercourse when one of the people is married.

**Exodus 20:15**
*Thou shalt not commit adultery.*

*Sex Lesson #2*

**B  Is Fornication Sin?**                                                                                     Yes

**1 Corinthians 6:13**
*... Now the body is not for fornication, but for the Lord; and the Lord for the body.*

Fornication is any type of sexual sin. Generally is it sex between two unmarried people. Even if they are engaged to get married.

**C  Is Prostitution Sin?**                                                                                    Yes

**1 Corinthians 6:15**
*Know ye not that your bodies are the members of Christ? Shall I then take the members of Christ, and make them the members of an harlot? GOD FORBID. (Emphasis added)*

Prostitution is when sex is provided for money (or other value). The woman is called a prostitute, harlot or whore.

**Notes:**
_____
_____
_____
_____
_____
_____
_____

## D. Is Masturbation Sin?            Yes

Masturbation is artificial stimulation of the penis or vagina. It is an uncleanness.

**Leviticus 15:16**
*And if any man's **seed of copulation** go out from him, then he shall wash all his flesh in water, and be unclean until the evening.*

'Seed of copulation' refers to semen from the penis.

**Deuteronomy 23:10**
*If there be among you any man, that is not clean by reason of uncleanness that chanceth him by night (wet dream), then shall he go abroad out of the camp..."*

'Chanceth him by night' is when the seed of copulation is accidentally ejaculated during a wet dream.

## E  Is Oral Sex Sin? Anal Sex?         Yes

**Romans 1:24**
*Wherefore God also gave them up to uncleanness through the lusts of their own hearts, to dishonour their own bodies between themselves.*

The dishonouring of the body is sin. The penis is for the vagina, not for the mouth or the rectum. Neither is the mouth for the vagina, penis or rectum.

(This scripture refers to sinful sexual practices.)

Sex Lesson #2

### F  Is Homosexuality Sin? Lesbianism?     Yes

God makes it very clear. Sodomy is a abomination.

**Leviticus 20:13**
*If a man also lie with mankind, as he lieth with a woman, both of them have committed an abomination.*

Abomination means "disgusting." A stench to God.

**Deuteronomy 24:17**
*There shall be no whore of the daughters of Israel, nor a sodomite of the sons of Israel.*

God said this in the time of Moses, but he speaks of it again after Jesus' resurrection.

**Genesis 19:7-8  7**
*And said, 'I pray you, brethren, do not so wickedly.*

*8 Behold now, I have two daughters which have not known man; let me, I pray you, bring them out unto you, and do ye to them as is good in your eyes: only unto these men do nothing; for therefore came they under the shadow of my roof.*

What this is really saying is that these men were so sinful that they even preferred men over women.

**Romans 1:26-27**
*26 For this cause God gave them up unto **vile affections:** for even their women did change the natural use into that which is **against nature.***

God calls lesbianism (women with women) a "vile affection" and against nature.

*27 And likewise also the men,* **leaving the natural use of the woman,** *burned in their lust one toward another; men with men* **working that which is unseemly,** *and receiving in themselves that recompence of the error which was meet.*

**Ephesians 5:12**
*For it is a shame to even speak of those things which are done of them in secret.*

God calls homosexuality "leaving the natural use of the woman".

"Recompense" is a penalty they received — the word does not say what kind. (perhaps something comparable to Herpes or AIDS)

Today they have come out of the closet and claimed it an "alternative life style."

## G. Is Incest Sin?                                                                 Yes

**Leviticus 18:6-16**
*(Summarized) None of you shall approach to any that is* **near of kin** *to him, to uncover their nakedness: I am the LORD. The nakedness of thy father...thy mother...thy step mother...thy sister..thy step sister...thy son's daughter (granddaughter) ...thy daughter's daughter ... thy father's sister (aunt)...thy mother's sister (aunt)...thy father's brother's wife (aunt)...thy brother's wife (sister-in-law).*

**Notes:**

God is saying no sex with, or marriage to, any close relative or in-law.

*Sex Lesson #2*

**H  Is Sex With Both A Mother & Her Daughter Sin?**  **Yes**

It is sinful for you to have sex with women who are themselves near of kin. (The same applies for a woman with both a man and his son.)

**Leviticus 18:23**
*Thou shalt not uncover the nakedness of a woman and her daughter, neither shalt thou take her son's daughter, or her daughter's daughter to uncover her nakedness; for they are her **near kinswomen**: it is wickedness.*

**J  Is Sex With Animals Sin?**  **Yes**

It is a sin to have sex with an animal. It really takes a depraved person to join his body with that of an animal.

**Leviticus 18:23**
*Neither shalt thou lie with any beast to defile thyself therewith: neither shall any woman stand before a beast to lie down thereto...*

**Notes:**
_____
_____
_____
_____

*The Basic Facts of Life*

## VII Is Abortion Sin?                                     Yes

**Luke 1:39,41** *39 And Mary arose in those days, and went into the hill country with haste, into a city of Juda*

*41 And it came to pass, that, when Elisabeth heard the salutation of Mary, the babe leaped in her womb*

This shows two things: First, the baby in Elisabeth's womb was alive. Second, it recognized in its spirit the presence of Mary.

**Genesis 25:21-24**
*21 And Rebekah his wife conceived.*

*22 And the children struggled together within her; and she said, "If it be so, why am I thus?" And she went to enquire of the LORD.*

*23 And the LORD said unto her, "Two nations are in thy womb, and the two manner of people shall be separated from thy bowels; and the one people shall be stronger than the other people; and the elder shall serve the younger."*

*24 And when her days to be delivered were fulfilled (nine months over), behold, there were twins in her womb.*

It is clear from this that the personalities in babies has started in the mother's womb. They were fighting. They were alive.

**Notes:**

*Sex Lesson #2*

**Exodus 21:22**
*If men strive, and hurt a woman with child, so that her fruit depart from her, and yet no mischief follow: he shall be surely punished, according as the woman's husband will lay upon him; and he shall pay as the judges determine.'*

With child' means pregnant. 'Hurt' is equivalent to abort. 'Fruit' is baby fetus.

God requires punishment for abortion.

**Psalms 139:13**
*For thou hast covered me in my mother's womb.*

Our spirits are covered with flesh in our mother's womb.

**Hebrews 7:9-10**
*9 And as I may so say, Levi also, who receiveth tithes, payed tithes in Abraham.*

*10 For he was yet in the loins of his father, when Melchisedec met him.*

The phrase 'in the loins' means in his body.

This describes even a pre-conception existence of man when his seed is yet in his great-grandfather.

This makes scientific sense. Science tells us that matter can neither be created nor destroyed, it only exists in another form.

**Notes:**
_____
_____
_____

## VIII  Abortion Is Sacrifice To Idol Gods

In ancient days Satan deceived people to sacrifice their sons and daughters to a god called Molech. A common practice of many nations, he deceived the Israelites to do the same thing.

Today, he is more subtle. He gets people to sacrifice their unborn sons and daughters in the name of abortion. He enjoys the sacrifice as it mocks God.

**Leviticus 20:2**
*Again, thou shalt say to the children of Israel, "Whosoever he be of the children of Israel, or of the strangers that sojourn in Israel, that giveth any of his seed unto Molech; he shall surely be put to death: The people of the land shall stone him with stones.*

'Seed' refers to child, either born or unborn.

## Sex Lesson #2

### Scriptural References for Sex Lesson No. 2
### (This list may be reproduced for your son or daughter.)

**What & who is sexual intercourse for?**
Gen 4:1 Adam knew Eve his wife...she conceived, and bare Cain
Prov 5:18 Let thy fountain be blessed: and rejoice ...

**Virginity is important to Marriage.**
Heb 9:18 neither the first testament was dedicated without blood
Heb 9:19 he took the blood of....and sprinkled both the book...
Heb 9:20 blood of the testament which God had enjoined unto you.
Mk 14:24 This is my blood of the new testament, which is shed...
Deut 22:13-29 (Old testament laws regarding virginity test)
Gen 2:24 shall cleave unto his wife...shall be one flesh.

**Adultery is sin.**
Exo 20:15 Thou shalt not commit adultery.

**Fornication is sin.**
1 Cor 6:13 Now the body is not for fornication, but for the Lord..

**Prostitution is sin.**
1 Cor 6:15 and make them the members of an harlot?  God forbid.

**Masturbation is sin.**
Lev 15:16 seed of copulation of out him, the he ...be unclean...
Deut 23:10 uncleanness that chanceth him by night...

**Oral or anal sex is sin.**
Rom 1:24 up to uncleanness..to dishonour their own bodies...

**Homosexuality or lesbianism is sin.**
Lev 20:13 lie with mankind...have committed an abomination...
Deut 24:17 Shall be no whore...sodomite of the sons of Israel.
Gen 19:7 I pray you, brethren, do not so wickedly.
Gen 19:8 two daughters...unto you...unto these men do nothing..
Rom 1:26 God gave them up unto vile affections...against nature
Rom 1:27 leaving the natural use of the woman...which is...

**Incest is sin.**
Lev 18:6-16 None of you shall approach any that is near of kin..

**Sex with both a mother and her daughter is sin.**
Lev 18:23 shalt not uncover...near kinswomen; it is wickedness.

**Sex with animals is sin.**
Lev 18:23 Neither ... lie with any beast to defile thyself.

**Abortion is sin.**
Lk 1:39-41 the babe leaped in her womb...
Gen 25:21 And Rebekah his wife conceived.
Gen 25:22 And the children struggled together within her...
Gen 25:23 LORD said unto her, Two nations are in thy womb...
Gen 25:24 behold, there were twins in her womb.
Exo 21:22 hurt a woman with child...shall be surely punished...
Heb 7:9 Levi also ... payed tithes in Abraham.
Heb 7:10 For he was yet in the loins of his father...

**Abortion is sacrifice to idol gods**
Lev 20:2 giveth any of his seed unto Molech...put to death..

*Overview*
*Sex Lesson No. 3*

# How Sexual Temptations Come

The last time we got together we talked about the Basic Facts of Life. Today we will be talking about How Sexual Temptations Come.

There is a definite pattern to temptation, whether it is for sex, drugs, murder or any work of the flesh. This is the basic message you should get today:

      I Temptation Targets Lust & Pride.

     II God hates pride.

    III There is a Law of Sin and Death in your members.

    IV Satan is disguised as an "Angel of light."

     V Satan is a fallen angel.

    VI Spiritual weapons are used against you.

   VII You will be tempted.

  VIII Their weapons won't prosper.

*Sex Lesson #3*

## I Temptation Targets Lust & Pride

Eve was tempted the same way all men are tempted. Lust of the flesh, followed by lust of the eyes and then they act on pride.

**Genesis 2:15-17**
*15 And the LORD God took the man, and put him into the garden of Eden to dress it and to keep it.*

*16 And the LORD God commanded the man, saying, 'Of every tree of the garden thou mayest freely eat:*

*17 But of the tree of the knowledge of good and evil, thou shalt not eat of it: for in the day that thou eatest thereof thou shalt surely die.*

God makes it clear. If he eats of the tree, Adam will die in the day he eats of it.

**Genesis 3:1-6**
*1 Now the serpent was more subtil than any beast of the field which the Lord God had made. And he said unto the woman, "Yea, hath God said, 'Ye shall not eat of every tree of the garden?' "*

The first thing Satan did was to question the word of God, saying, "Yea, hath God said..."

*2 And the woman said unto the serpent, "We may eat of the fruit of the trees of the garden:*

Eve makes a mistake by discussing it with him.

## How Sexual Temptations Come

*3 But of the fruit of the tree which is in the midst of the garden, God hath said, 'Ye shall not eat of it, neither shall ye touch it, lest ye die.' "*

*4 And the serpent said unto the woman, **'Ye shall not surely die:***

*5 For God doth know that in the day ye eat thereof, then your eyes shall be opened, and **ye shall be as gods,** knowing good from evil.'*

*6 And when the woman saw that the tree was **good for food,** and that it was **pleasant to the eyes,** and a tree to be **desired to make one wise,** she took of the fruit thereof, and did eat, and gave also unto her husband with her; and he did eat.*

For some reason, Eve adds something to the word of God saying, 'Neither shall ye touch it...'

**Second,** Satan calls God a liar, saying 'Ye shall not surely die.'

**Third,** Satan appeals to Eve's desire for power by telling her she would 'be as gods.'

(How dumb! She and Adam were already told by God to have dominion over the earth. Genesis 1:28)

Adam was **not** deceived. He simply rebelled.

(Because everybody else was doing it?)

1. First he **questions the word of God?** "Hath God said...?" He is trying to make the victim **doubt** the word. For some reason she appears **confused.**

2. Next, he says the word of God is not true, that **God is a liar!**

(Have your son read 1 John 2:16 before you give him the third point.)

*Sex Lesson #3*

**1 John 2:16**
*For all that is in the world, the **lust of the flesh,** and the **lust of the eyes** and the **pride of life** is not of the Father, but is of the world.*

3. And lastly as a result of this, he appeals to Eve's

- Lust of her flesh (good for food)
- Lust of her eyes (pleasant to the eyes)
- Her pride of life (Desired for wisdom power)

**Lust of the eyes** can include all senses — the **ear gate,** the **nose gate,** the **taste gate** and the **touch gate.**

## II God Hates Pride

This is extremely important, son. God hates pride because it exalts man, not God. Would you read Proverbs 16:18.

**Proverbs 16:18**
*Pride goeth before destruction, and a haughty spirit before a fall.*

**2 Corinthians 10:5**
*Casting down imaginations, and every high thing that exalteth itself against the knowledge of God...*

Many people fall into sexual sin because of pride. They feel hurt, embarrassed or challenged by what someone says.

And the only way they see to save face is to show **their** power. They sin.

## III The Law of Sin & Death Is In Your Members

**Romans 8:21-23**

*21 I find then a law, that, **when I would do good, evil is present with me.***

Even when man wills to do good evil is working against him.

*22 For I delight in the **law of God** after the **inward man:***

**Inward man** refers to his spirit.

*23 But I see **another law** in my members, **warring against the law of my mind,** and bringing me into captivity to the **law of sin** which is **in my members.***

God revealed a **law in his flesh.** (Paul, the writer)

**The law of sin and death** entered man when Adam obeyed Satan (through Eve).

## Your Spirit Is Willing, But Your Flesh Is Weak!

Son, I know that in your heart you really do want to please God. But I also know that your body (will) wants to do what they say "comes natural."

**Matthew 26:41**
*Watch and pray, that ye enter not into temptation: **the spirit indeed is willing, but the flesh is weak.***

**Galatians 5:17**
*For the **flesh lusteth against the spirit,** and **the spirit against the flesh,** and these are **contrary (warring) the one to the other:** so that ye cannot do the things that you would.*

Your body and spirit are fighting each other.

Sex Lesson #3

## IV. Does Satan Come In A Red Suit With A Pitch Fork?   No

**2 Corinthians 11:13-14**
*13 For such are false apostles, deceitful workers, transforming themselves into the apostles of Christ.*

*14 And no marvel; for Satan himself is transformed into an "Angel of Light."*
(emphasis added)

Everybody would recognize him if he did. Satan disguises himself into what the Bible calls an "Angel of Light", pretending to "help" you.

## V. Satan Is A Fallen Angel

**Isaiah 14:12-17**
*12 How art thou fallen from heaven, O Lucifer, son of the morning! How art thou cut down to the ground, which didst weaken the nations!*

*13 For thou hast said in thine heart, I will ascend into heaven, I will exalt my throne above the stars of God: I will sit also upon the mount of the congregation, in the sides of the north:*

(If your son doesn't know the origin of Satan, this will help.)

Son, Satan (originally called Lucifer) is a fallen angel. He rebelled against God and tried to take over from God. We see this in Isaiah.

Satan was called Lucifer before he rebelled against God.

He tried to take over from God. God's seat is in the sides of the north.

*14 I will ascend above the heights of the clouds; I will be like the most High.*

*17 That made the world as a wilderness, and destroyed the cities thereof...*

The world was destroyed when God crushed Satan.

**Genesis 1:1-2**
*1 In the beginning God created the heaven and the earth,*

Genesis 1:1 tells us about the original creation.

*2 And the earth was without form, and void; and darkness was upon the face of the deep. And the spirit of God moved upon the face of the waters.*

Genesis 1:3 and following verses tell us about the "recreation" of the earth after it was destroyed when Satan rebelled.

**2 Peter 2:4**
*For if God spared not the angels that sinned, but cast them down to hell, and delivered them into chains of darkness, to be reserved unto judgment;*

The angels that rebelled with Satan were also cast down into hell.

**1 John 3:8**
*He that committeth sin is of the devil; for the devil sinneth from the beginning. For this purpose the Son of God was manifested, that he might destroy the works of the devil.*

But when Adam sinned, evil came back into the world. And Jesus came to undo Satan's works.

**Notes:**

## Sex Lesson #3

### VI Spiritual Weapons Are Used Against You

God lists in the Bible seven things that he hates. All of these are used against you to make you lust in your flesh, lust in your eyes or have pride in your life. Let's take a look at them. (Read all the scriptures before commenting.)

"Abomination" means disgusting — a "stench".

**Proverbs 6:16-19**
*16 These six things doth the LORD hate: yea seven are an abomination unto him:*

*17 A proud look, a lying tongue, and hands that shed innocent blood.*

*18 A heart that deviseth wicked imaginations, feet that be swift in running to mischief,*

*19 A false witness that speaketh lies, and he that soweth discord among brethren.*

1. PRIDE. Pride is putting "self" before God. Eve fell after her pride was tested.

2. LIES — To People. Satan lied to Eve saying she would not die.

3. MURDER. (1 John 3:15 says, 'Whosoever hateth his brother is a murderer.')

4. HEARTS DEVISING WICKED IMAGINATION

5. PEOPLE LOOKING FOR TROUBLE

6. PEOPLE LYING AGAINST PEOPLE (false witness)

## How Sexual Temptations Come

**Proverbs 2:16**
*To deliver thee from the strange woman, even from the stranger which flattereth with her words.*

**Proverbs 7:21**
*With her much fair speech she caused him to yield, with the flattering of her lips she forced him.*

7. MALICIOUS GOSSIPERS

God also hates the following:

8. FLATTERY — Deceitful praise. Men and women often use it to soften up the other to enter into sexual sin. It can either be a lie or the truth used for a deceitful purpose.

When people flatter, at least in your mind you should wonder, "What do they want?" If they want attention, what kind?"

(At this point, you may go to Sex Lesson No. 7 and read him a few examples of how "Angels of Light" work. I suggest not more than two or three examples.)

### VII Are There Other Ways You Can Be Tempted?    Yes

There is one straight line between two points, but many crooked lines. The people of the world can always find another way to tempt you. They will try to make you doubt the word of God, get you confused or make you fear.

**Luke 16:8**
*For the children of this world are in their generation wiser than the children of light.*

Children of this world means the "natural man" who follows Satan.

Children of light means the "spiritual man" who follows Christ.

Their generation is in the flesh til they die. Our generation is in the spirit forever.

*Sex Lesson #3*

## VIII Their Weapons Will Not Prosper

One very important thing about the word of God is that it will not allow the weapons used against you to prosper.

I will show you how to handle these and any situation in the 5th lesson. But for now, lets look at a key scripture on your power.

**Isaiah 54:17**
*No weapon that is formed against thee shall prosper; and every tongue that shall rise against thee in judgment thou shalt condemn. This is the heritage of the servants of the LORD, and their righteousness is of me, saith the LORD.*

Closing Comment: In Sex Lesson No. 4, I will start to show you how to fight these sexual temptation, using Jesus as the model of winning. To get you ready for that, I suggest you read the fourth chapter of Luke, verses 1 through 13.

## Scriptural References for Sex Lesson No. 3
(This list may be reproduced for your son or daughter.)

**Sin follows lust and pride.**
Gen 2:15 and put him into the garden of Eden to dress it...
Gen 2:16 every tree of the garden thou mayest freely eat...
Gen 2:17 the knowledge of good and evil, thou shalt not eat...
Gen 3:1 the serpent...Yea, hath God said...?
Gen 3:2 the woman said unto the serpent, We may eat of every...
Gen 3:3 But ... of the tree...not eat...neither...touch...
Gen 3:4 serpent said...Ye shall not surely die.
Gen 3:5 ye shall be as gods, knowing good from evil.
Gen 3:6 good...food, pleasant to eyes, desired to make...wise...
1 Jn 2:16 Lust of the flesh...eyes, pride of life...of the world.

**Why God hates pride.**
Prov 16:18 Pride goeth before destruction...
2 Cor 10:5 Casting down...every high thing that exalteth itself...

**The Law of sin and death is in your members.**
Rom 8:21 when I would do good, evil is present with me.
Rom 8:22 I delight in the law of God after the inward man.
Rom 8:23 law in my members, warring against the law of my...

**Your Spirit is willing, but your flesh is weak.**
Mt 26:41 The spirit is indeed willing, but the flesh is weak.
Gal 5:17 flesh lusteth against the spirit...spirit against...

**Satan transforms himself into an angel of light.**
2 Cor 11:13 false apostles...transforming themselves into the ...
2 Cor 11:14 Satan himself is transformed into an angel of light.

**Satan is a fallen angel.**
Isa 14:12 O Lucifer...How art thou cut down to the ground...
Isa 14:13 Thou hast said...I will...exalt my throne above...God...
Isa 14:14 I will be like the most High.
Isa 14:17 made the world as a wilderness...destroyed the cities.
Gen 1:1 In the beginning God created the heaven and the earth.
Gen 1:2 And the earth was without form, and void; and...
Gen 1:3 And God said, Let there be...
2 Pet 2:4 God spared not the angels that sinned, but cast them...
1 Jn 3:8 for the devil sinneth from the beginning...

**Spiritual weapons are used against you.**
Prov 6:16 the LORD hate: yea seven are an abomination unto him:
Prov 6:17 a proud look, a lying tongue...shed innocent blood...
Prov 6:18 heart that deviseth wicked imaginations, feet...swift...
Prov 6:19 false witness, soweth discord among brethren.
Prov 2:16 from the stranger which flattereth with her words.
Prov 7:21 much fair speech she caused him to yield...

**There are other ways you can be tempted.**
Lk 16:8 children of this world...wiser than the children of light.

**Their weapons won't prosper.**
Isa 54:17 No weapon that is formed against thee shall prosper...

*Overview*
*Sex Lesson No. 4*

# Jesus — The Role Model For Overcoming

The last time we got together we talked about How Sexual Temptations Come. Today we will look at how Jesus won his battle against Satan in the Wilderness.

    I The battle is spiritual, not physical.

    II Jesus in battle against Satan in the wilderness.

    III Jesus prepared for his ministry.

    IV How Jesus won against Satan.

    V You can win the way Jesus won.

    VI Some precautions to take:

        1 Examine yourself

        2 Preparation through meditation

        3 Execution by the Holy Spirit - Not from memory

        4 Don't show off scriptural knowledge

## Lesson #4

5  Don't try to teach or correct non-Christian tempters.

6  Be wise in correcting Christian tempters.

### I  Is the Battle Against People?   No

**Ephesians 6:12**
*For we wrestle not against flesh and blood...but against principalities...*

*against powers....*

The fight is not against people. Eve got deceived by Satan and then got Adam to sin.

*against the rulers of the darkness of this world...*

*Against spiritual wickedness in high places.*

These are the various type of demonic spirits that tempt people to sin.

### II  How Jesus Fought With The Word of God

*Testing Jesus for **Lust of the Flesh***

**Luke 4:2-4**
*2 Being forty days tempted of the devil. And in those days he did eat nothing: and when they were ended, he afterward hungered.*

*3 And the devil said unto him, "If thou be the Son of God, command this stone that it be made bread."*

Now we can take a look at how Jesus, himself, won a battle with Satan in the wilderness. Would you read verses 2 through 3 of the 4th chapter of Luke. Then I will make some comments:

Several comments on this:

• **Jesus ignored Satan's temptations** until his fast was over.

• Jesus was hungry so Satan was **testing for lust of his flesh.**

*4 And Jesus answered him, saying, "It is written, 'That man shall not live by bread alone, but by every word of God.'"*

- **If Jesus obeys** him at any point, Satan becomes his God.

- Satan questions Jesus, seemingly trying **to make him doubt** he is the Son of God.

- Jesus answers with the word of God from Deuteronomy 8:3. (you may have your son look it up there)

- Jesus wins the preliminaries and the first round.

---

*Testing Jesus for*
**Lust of the Eyes**

---

**Luke 4:5-8**
*5 And the devil, taking him up into an high mountain, **shewed unto him** all the kingdoms of the world in a moment of time.*

*6 And the devil said unto him, "All this power will I give thee, and the glory of them: for that is delivered unto me; and to whomsoever I will give it.*

*7 If thou therefore wilt worship me, all shall be thine.*

*8 And Jesus answered and said unto him, "Get thee behind me, Satan: For it is written, 'Thou shalt worship the Lord thy God, and him only shalt thou serve.'"*

In this temptation, Satan asks Jesus for exactly what he wants. He wants Jesus to worship him.

Several Points to Be Made:

- Satan is testing Jesus for lust in his eyes. (*shewed unto him")

- Satan was trying to tempt Jesus with what God had already promised him.

- Jesus quoted him Deuteronomy 6:13. (Have your son look up and read this.)

Sex Lesson #4

## Testing Jesus for *Pride of Life*

**Luke 4:9-13**

9 And he brought him to Jerusalem, and set him on a pinnacle of the temple, and said unto him, "If thou be the Son of God, cast thyself down from hence:

10 For it is written, 'He shall give his angels charge over thee, to keep thee:

11 And in their hands they shall bear thee up, lest at any time thou dash thy foot against a stone.'"

12 And Jesus answering said unto him, "It is said, 'Thou shalt not tempt the Lord thy God."

13 And when the devil had ended all the temptation, he departed from him for a season.

**Notes:**

In the next test, Satan is testing for any pride Jesus might have in the word of God.

- **Now Satan is quoting scripture to Jesus.** (You should have your son look up and read Psalms 91:11-12.)

- Satan is **still trying to make Jesus doubt who he is,** saying, 'If thou be the Son of God.'

- Satan is trying to get Jesus to act foolishly. (Just like people might say, 'If your God meets all your needs, jump out of a 35 floor office building and prove it.')

- **Jesus once again uses the word of God** quoting Deuteronomy 6:16. (You should have your son look up and read it, too.)

## III Did Jesus Prepare For His Ministry?   Yes

(Your son needs to know that the man, Jesus, prepared for his ministry with the word of God, just as he is to study the word of God.)

**Philippians 2:6-7**
6 *Who, being in the form of God, thought it not robbery to be equal with God:*

7 *But made himself of no reputation, and took upon him the form of a servant, and was made in the likeness of men.*

Jesus made himself as man so he could offer the blood of a perfect man to redeem mankind.

**Luke 2:40**
*And the child grew, and waxed strong in spirit, filled with wisdom: and the grace of God was upon him.*

Jesus is a growing child in Luke 2:40. He is growing in the word.

**Luke 2:46-47**
46 *And it came to pass, that after three days they found him in the temple, sitting in the midst of the doctors, **both hearing them, and asking them questions.***

47 *And all that heard him were astonished at **his understanding and answers.***

And though Jesus is still growing at age 12, his knowledge impresses the experts in Jerusalem.

## Sex Lesson #4

**Luke 4:16-17**
*16 And he came to Nazareth, where he had been brought up; and,* **as his custom was,** *he went into the synagogue on the sabbath day, and* **stood up for to read.**

*17 And there was delivered unto him the book of the prophet Esaias.*

At age 30, Jesus starts his ministry, reading the scroll as had been his custom at Nazareth.

### IV How Jesus Won The Battle

(As an introduction to how your son wins his battles, I suggest you simply summarize how and why Jesus won this battle.)

1. Jesus knew he was the Son of God.
2. Jesus put God first.
3. Jesus ignored Satan's initial temptations.
4. Jesus fought with the word of God.

**Notes**
_____
_____
_____
_____

## V  How Your Son Wins His Battles

**John 14:12-14**

*12 Verily, verily, I say unto you, He that believeth on me, the works that I do shall he do also; and greater works than these shall he do; because I go unto my Father.*

*13 And whatsoever ye shall ask in my name, that will I do, that the Father may be glorified in the Son.*

*14 If ye shall ask anything in my name, I will do it.*

**John 1:12**

*But as many as received him, to them gave he power to become the* **sons of God,** *even to them that believe on his name.*

("Ask" means demand.)

Son, this means that you can win your battles doing what Jesus did to win his battle.

(You may want to go back over how Jesus won.)

1. You must remember that you are the temple of the Holy Spirit.

2. You must put God first. (See Lesson No. 6 for how to put God first.)

3. You should ignore temptations when possible.

4. You must fight with the word of God, both scriptures and commands such as "In the name of Jesus, NO!"

We will cover more of this in Sex Lesson No. 7.

*Sex Lesson #4*

## VI Some Precautions to Take

There are a some very important precautions you should take. We will talk about each one. They are:

1. Examine yourself.

2. Preparation through meditation.

3. Execution by the Holy Spirit - Not from memory.

4. Don't show off scriptural knowledge.

5. Don't try to teach or correct non-Christian tempters.

6. Be wise in correcting Christian tempters.

## 1 Examine Yourself

Sometimes you can be your worst enemy. By some act of disobedience to the word of God, you can bring temptation to yourself. Some examples could include:

- Unequal yoking with unbelievers. (the wrong crowd)

## Jesus — The Role Model For Overcoming

**1 Corinthians 11:28, 31**
*28 But let a man examine himself...*

*31 For if we would judge ourselves, we should not be judged.*

- Drugs, drunkenness
- Lying (Trying maybe to make people believe you have had sex.)
- Disobedience to God, your parents, other authorities.

If you find out you have sinned, judge the sin and ask God to forgive you.

### 2. Preparation through Meditation

(The following scriptures will help your son understand why knowing the word of God is important.)

1. You will prosper and have good success.

**Joshua 1:8**
*This book of the law shall not depart out of thy mouth; but thou shalt meditate therein day and night, that thou mayest observe to do according to all that is written therein: for then thou shalt make thy way prosperous, and then thou shalt have good success.*

Meditating on the word gets it deep into your spirit.

*Sex Lesson #4*

2. You will have a defense against the devil.

**Ephesians 6:10-11**
*10 Finally, my brethren, **be strong in the Lord,** and in the power of his might.*
*11 Put on the whole armour of God, that ye may be able to stand against the wiles of the devil.*

To be 'strong in the Lord' is to be strong in the scriptures. This is similar to the way that Jesus 'waxed strong.'

'Wiles of the devil' is the trickery and deception of the devil.

3. You will have an offense against the devil.

**Ephesians 6:17**
*And take the helmet of salvation, and **the sword of the Spirit,** which is the word of God.*

In the same way that Jesus told Satan to 'Get thee behind me,' you can tell demons to flee 'In the name of Jesus.'

**Mark 16:17**
*And these signs shall follow them that believe; In my name shall they cast out devils..*

You only have to do two things —Believe and Speak to them.

**John 14:12**
*Verily, verily, I say unto you, He that believeth on me, the works that I do shall he do also; and greater works than these shall he do; because I go unto my Father.*

Jesus told us to use his power.

## 3. Execute By the Unction of the Holy Spirit—Not From Memory

**Matthew 10:19-20**
*19 Take no thought how or what ye shall speak: for it shall be given you in that same hour what ye shall speak.*

When the word of God is planted in your heart, the Holy Spirit will bring it to your remembrance.

*20 For it is not ye that speak, but the Spirit of your Father which speaketh in you.*

The Spirit is actually using you to speak.

**John 14:26**
*But the Comforter, which is the Holy Ghost, whom the Father will send in my name, he shall teach you all things, and bring all things to your remembrance, whatsoever I have said unto you.*

**Psalms 119:11,15-16**
*11 Thy word have I **hid in mine heart,** that I might not sin against thee.*

When you meditate on the words of God, they are planted deep in your heart.

*15 I will meditate in thy precepts, and have respect unto thy ways.*

*16 I will delight myself in thy statutes: I will not forget thy word.*

*Sex Lesson #4*

## 4. Do Not Show Off Scriptural Knowledge

**Matthew 6:1**
*Take heed that ye do not your alms before men, **to be seen of them:** otherwise ye have no reward of your Father which is in heaven.*

To show off how much scripture you know is pride. God hates pride and will not honor your boasting. He wants the glory.

## 5. Do Not Try to Teach or Correct Non-Christians

To correct a natural man is a disaster waiting to happen. Don't do it.

**1 Corinthians 1:20**
*For the preaching of the cross is to them that perish foolishness; but unto us which are saved it is the power of God.*

1. It is foolishness to them. They wouldn't understand.

**1 Corinthians 2:14**
*But the natural man receiveth not the things of the Spirit of God: for they are foolishness unto him: neither can he know them, because they are spiritually discerned.*

**Matthew 7:6**
*Give not that which is holy unto the dogs, neither cast ye your pearls before swine, lest they trample them under their feet, and turn again and rend you.*

**Proverbs 9:6-7**
*6 Forsake the foolish and live...*

*7 He that reproveth a scorner getteth to himself shame: and he that rebuketh a wicked man getteth himself a blot.*

2. They will trample on the word and turn on you.

Jesus uses 'swine' and 'dogs' as another word for the natural man.

The word says to leave fools alone, you'll get hit.

## 6. Be Wise In Correcting Christians Who Tempt You

**2 Timothy 3:16**
*All scripture is given by inspiration of God, and is for doctrine, for reproof, for correction, for instruction in righteousness.*

**James 4:15**
*But speaking the truth in love...*

**Proverbs 9:8**
*Rebuke a wise man and he will love thee.*

To correct a Christian depends on how mature he is. If he is really wise, he will accept it. If he is a baby Christian, he may behave as the natural man.

Correction must be done in love. The statement, rebuke in private, praise in public would apply.

(I would then suggest you read to him the following scripture which describes the baby Christian.)

*Sex Lesson #4*

**1 Corinthians 3:3**
For ye are yet carnal: for whereas there is among you envying, and strife, and divisions, are ye not carnal, and walk as men.

As you can see son, some Christians act just like the natural man. You should ask the Holy Spirit whether you should correct them or not.

**Reading Assignment For Next Lesson:**

In the Sex Lesson No. 5, I will show more on how to fight sexual sin, this time by looking at two men who were tempted. I want you to read about them in advance.

The Story of Joseph & Potiphar's Wife
    Genesis 39.    Read the entire chapter.
               (Chapters 37, 40 through 50 Optional)

The Tragedy of Amnon and Tamar
    2 Samuel 13.    Read the entire chapter.

*Jesus — The Role Model For Overcoming*

## Scriptural References for Sex Lesson No. 4
(This list may be reproduced for your son or daughter.)

**The Battle is spiritual**
Eph 6:12 For we wrestle not against flesh and blood, but against...

**Jesus Fought Satan with the word of God**
Lk 4:2 forty days tempted of the devil...afterward hungered...
Lk 4:3 If thou be the Son of God...stone that it be made bread...
Lk 4:4 It is written...not by bread alone...by every word of God...
Deut 8:3 not by bread alone...every word that proceedeth out...
Lk 4:5 the devil...shewed unto him all the kingdoms of the world...
Lk 4:6 All this power will I give thee, and the glory of them...
Lk 4:7 If thou therefore wilt worship me, all shall be thine.
Lk 4:8 For it is written...thou shalt worship the Lord thy God...
Deut 6:13 Thou shalt fear the LORD thy God, and serve him...
Lk 4:9 thou be the Son of God, cast thyself down from hence.
Lk 4:10 For it is written, He shall give his angels charge over.
Lk 4:11 They shall bear thee up lest...thou dash thy foot...
Lk 4:12 It is said, thou shalt not tempt the Lord thy God.
Deut 6:16 Ye shall not tempt the LORD thy God...
Lk 4:13 the devil...departed from him for a season.

**Jesus prepared for his ministry.**
Phil 2:6 thought it not robbery to be equal with God...
Phil 2:7 made himself of no reputation..servant..likeness of men...
Lk 2:40 the child grew and waxed strong in spirit...
Lk 2:46 in the temple...both hearing them, and asking questions...
Lk 2:47 were astonished at his understanding and answers.
Lk 4:16 he went into the synagogue..stood up for to read...
Lk 4:17 delivered unto him the book of the prophet Esaias.

**How Jesus won the battle.**
1. Jesus knew he was the Son of God. 2. Jesus put God first. 3. Jesus ignored Satan's initial temptations. 4. Jesus fought with the word of God.

*Sex Lesson #4*

---

**How Your Son wins his battles. (Same as Jesus)**
Jn 14:12 he that believeth on me...greater works ...shall he do...
Jn 14:13 whatsoever ye shall ask in my name, that will I do...
Jn 14:14 If ye shall ask anything in my name, I will do it.
Jn 1:12 to them he gave power to be the sons of God...

**Examine yourself.**
1 Cor 11:28 But let a man examine himself...
1 Cor 11:31 if we would judge ourselves, we should not be judged...

**Preparation through meditation.**
Jos 1:8 but thou shalt meditate therein day and night...
Eph 6:10 Finally, my brethren, be strong in the Lord...
Eph 6:11 put on the whole armour of God, that ye may be able...
Eph 6:17 and the sword of the spirit, which is the word of God...
Mk 16:17 that believe; In my name shall they cast out devils...
Jn 14:12 greater works ...shall he do because I go to my Father...

**Execution by the Holy Spirit—Not from memory.**
Mt 10:19 Take no thought how or what ye shall speak for it...
Mt 10:20 For it is not ye that speak, but the Spirit...
Jn 14:26 and bring all things to your remembrance...
Psl 119:11 word have I hid in mine heart, that I might not sin...
Psl 119:15 I will meditate in thy precepts, and have respect...
Psl 119:16 I will delight myself in thy statutes...

**You should not show off scriptural knowledge.**
Mt 6:1 before men, to be seen of them...ye have no reward...

Do not teach or correct non-Christians.
1 Cor 1:20 the cross is to them that perish foolishness...
1 Cor 2:14 because they are spiritually discerned...
Mt 7:6 not that which is holy unto the dogs...before swine..
Prov 9:6 Forsake the foolish and live...
Prov 9:7 he that bebuketh a wicked man getteth himself a blot.

**Be careful in correcting a "Christian".**
2 Tim 3:16 All scripture...for correction...in righteousness.
Jas 4:15 But speaking the truth I love...
Prov 9:8 Rebuke a wise man and he will love thee.
1 Cor 3:3 are ye not carnal, and walk as men...

*Overview*
*Sex Lesson No. 5*

# Overcoming Peer & Other Pressure

In the last lesson, I taught you about Jesus as The Role Model for Overcoming. Today we will be looking at the stories you had in your homework assignment. After that we will start to talk more specifically about how you apply the word of God and overcome in your life.

    I  The example of Amnon and Tamar

    II  The example of Joseph and Potiphar's wife

    III  A comparison of the two examples with Jesus

    IV  How God blesses obedience

## Sex Lesson #5

### I Amnon Rapes Tamar

**Note to the Father:** (The following questions should stimulate discussion on how Amnon was tempted. Make sure he has read the entire 13th Chapter of 2 Samuel. This lesson won't mean much without it.)

Son, let's take a look at how Amnon came to rape Tamar. In this lesson, you will see how Amnon had himself all set up to fall and how Jonadab came to push him over the ledge. You will see many spiritual forces at work.

We will be doing this by question and answer. You can refer to your Bible for the answers. THIS IS NOT A TEST.

1. How were the following related?

    a. Absalom & Tamar _____ (brother/sister - vs. 1)

    b. Amnon & Tamar _____ (half brother/sister - vs. 2)

    c. Jonadab & Amnon _____ (first cousins)

2. Who was in love with Tamar? _____ (Amnon - vs. 1)

3. Did Amnon think he could have Tamar?
    _____ (Not at first vs. 2)

4. Who was the Angel of Light? _____ (Jonadab - vs. 3)

5. What word describes Jonadab? _____ (subtle - vs. 3)

6. Whose heart deviseth wicked imagination?
    _____ (Jonadab)

7. Whose feet were swift in running to mischief?
    _____ (Jonadab)
    _____ (Absalom)

8. Who had a lying tongue to King David?
    _____ (Amnon)

9. Who soweth discord among the brethren?
   _____ (Jonadab)

10. Who committed murder?
    _____ (Absalom)
    _____ (Amnon through hatred)

11. What word described the Serpent in the Garden? _____

12. What words in the scriptures show the following:

    a. Lust of the Flesh _____ (vexed, vs 2)

    b. Lust of the Eyes _____ (beautiful, vs 1)

    c. Pride of Life _____ (thou being the King's son, vs 4)

13. What kind of love did Amnon have for Tamar?
    _____ (Erotic)

14. Did Amnon love Tamar after he raped her? (No)

15. Was Anyone else around when Amnon raped Tamar? (No)

16. How did each of the following suffer?

    a. Amnon _____ (hated the woman he had loved)
    (hated by his half brother)
    (was murdered)

    b. Tamar _____ (remained desolate)
    (lost her virginity)

    c. Absalom _____ (hated his half brother)
    (had to flee from his home)

    d. King David _____ (angered by the rape)
    (one of his sons was murdered)
    (his daughter suffered mental anguish and disgrace)
    (one of his sons fled from home)

## Sex Lesson #5

17. Did Jonadab suffer?
    Yes.   No.

(No. At least not indicated by scripture. In fact, he appears from verse 32 through 35 that he was still serving the king.)

### II Potiphar's Wife Tries to Seduce Joseph

(These questions are designed to stimulate discussion on Joseph and Potiphar's wife. Portions of the scripture are included for your convenience, but not necessarily to be read.)

**Genesis 39**

7 ...**His master's wife cast her eyes upon Joseph; and she said, "Lie with me."**

8 But he refused, and said unto his master's wife, "Behold, my master wotteth not what is with me in the house, and he hath committed all that he hath to my hand;"

9 "There is none greater in this house than I; neither hath he kept back any thing from me but thee, because thou art his wife: **how then can I do this great wickedness, and sin against God?"**

10 And it came to pass, as **she spake to Joseph day by day,** that he hearkened not unto her, **to lie by her,** or **to be with her.**

11 And it came to pass about this time that Joseph went into the house to do his business; and there was none of the men of the house there within.

12 And she caught him by his garment, saying **"Lie with me:"** and he left his garment in her hand, and fled, and got him out.

17 And she spake unto him (her husband) "The Hebrew servant, which thou hast brought unto us, came in unto me to mock me.."

19 ... (her husband's) wrath was kindled.

20 And Joseph's master took, and **put him into the prison,** a place where the king's prisoners were bound: and he was there in prison.

21 **But the LORD** was with Joseph, and **shewed him mercy,** and gave him **favour in the sight of the keeper of the prison.**

Son, I will ask the questions again. If you wish, you can refer to your Bible for the answers.

1. Who had the lust? _____ (Potiphar's wife)

2. Who refused to make love? _____ (Joseph)

3. Why did he refuse? _____ (It was sin)

4. Did Potiphar's wife give up? _____ Yes _____ No  (No)

5. How did she change her tactic?
   _____ (constant pressure)
   _____ (a diversion for them to just
   _____ talk—"be with her")

6. Did she grab him while others were present?

   Yes    No    (No)

7. Did Joseph take advantage of being away from home?
   _____ Yes _____ No  (No)

8. Which required a stronger man?

   _____ To Lie With Her?
   _____ To Run Away From Her?

9. Who was a false witness? _____ (Potiphar's wife)

10. Did she really love him? Why do you answer the way you do.
    _____ Yes _____ No

11. What kind of love did she have for Joseph?
    _____ (erotic)

12. Did Joseph love her? If so, what kind? Why do you say that?

13. Whom did Joseph Love? _____ (God)

14. How was Joseph punished?
    _____ _____ (Prison)

*Sex Lesson #5*

15. Which did God do?

    \_\_\_\_\_ Protect Joseph? (Yes, masters usually castrated the sex organs of their house servants)

    \_\_\_\_\_ Punish Joseph? (No)

    \_\_\_\_\_ Reward Joseph? (Yes, favour in the prison)

## III A Comparison of Joseph and Amnon Examples To Jesus

(This comparison should start to nail down the fact that as Joseph overcame the temptations and pressures for sexual sin so can we. And we can overcome by standing on the word of God.)

| The conditions of the temptation | Jesus | Joseph | Amnon |
|---|---|---|---|
| 1 Rank order the difficulty of their temptations?<br>1 most difficult<br>2 next most<br>3 least | \_\_\_1 | \_\_\_2 | \_\_\_3 |
| 2. Which man was farthest away (physically) from his father? Second? Third? | \_\_\_1 | \_\_\_2 | \_\_\_3 |
| 3. Which men had no choice about their yoking? | \_\_\_x | \_\_\_x | \_\_\_ |

Notes:
_____
_____
_____
_____

## Their spiritual strength

|  | Jesus | Joseph | Amnon |
|---|---|---|---|
| 1. Which man knew who his God was? | ___x | ___x | ___ |
| 2. Which men resisted the temptation. | ___x | ___x | ___ |
| 3. Which man was weakened by lust of his flesh? | ___ | ___ | ___x |
| 4. Which man was weakened by lust of his eyes? | ___ | ___ | ___x |
| 5. Which man had favor with God? | ___x | ___x | ___ |
| 6. Which men defended themselves with the word of God? | ___x | ___x | ___ |

## The results

|  | Jesus | Joseph | Amnon |
|---|---|---|---|
| 1. Which men overcame the temptation(s)? | ___x | ___x | ___ |
| 2. Which man was murdered? (immediately) | ___ | ___ | ___x |
| 3. Which man's family was blessed? (*two of them) | ___x | ___x | ___ |
| 4. Which man's family was torn apart? | ___ | ___ | ___x |

Notes:

Sex Lesson #5

## IV How God Blesses Obedience

### Joseph's Family Was Blessed

It is important to note how Joseph's entire family was blessed, including his father and his eleven brothers.

**Genesis 47:5-6**
*5 And Pharaoh spake unto Joseph, saying, "Thy father and thy brethren are come unto thee:*

*6 The land of Egypt is before thee; in the **best of the land** make thy father and brethren to dwell; in the land of Goshen let them dwell: ...*

They were given not just land, but the 'best of the land.'

### Jesus' Family—The Church Is Blessed

**Ephesians 3:15**
*(Jesus) Of whom the whole family in heaven and earth is named.*

So for everyone who accepts Christ, he becomes a member of THE Family.

Those living and those who have died and gone to heaven.

**Ephesians 2:19**
*Now therefore ye are no more strangers and foreigners, but fellow citizens with the saints, and of the household of God.*

We are the household of God.

## Scriptural References for Sex Lesson No. 5
(This list may be reproduced for your son or daughter.)

**The story of Joseph and Potiphar's wife.**
Genesis 39 (the entire chapter)

**The tragedy of Amnon and Tamar.**
2 Samuel 13 (the entire chapter)

**Joseph's family was blessed.**
Gen 47:5 Thy father and thy brethren are come unto thee.
Gen 47:6 the best of the land...father and brethren to dwell.

**Jesus' family, the Church, is blessed.**
Eph 3:15 Of whom the whole family in heaven and earth is named.
Eph 2:19 fellow citizens with the ... household of God

*Overview*
*Sex Lesson No. 6*

## How to Follow God's Map

**Note:** The teaching pages for this lesson are in Pre-Marriage Lesson No. 6

---

The scriptures tell us that:

Without faith it is impossible to please God: for he that cometh to God must believe that he is and that he is a rewarder of them that diligently seek him. (Hebrews 11:4)

And since he rewards those who diligently seek him, I am going to tell you how to seek him. In essence, you have to HS-MAP which means to

H - Hear His Word
S - Study His Word
M - Meditate On His Word
A - Act On His Word
P - Pray Without Ceasing

Another way to remember this is to call it "His Map" without the "I" for Hear, Study, Meditate, Act and Pray.

Success in life comes when you put Jesus in the center of your life.

*Overview*
*Sex Lesson No. 7*

# *Becoming More Like Jesus*

This is the last lesson on sex. Today, we will be talking in three areas:

      I  Sword Fights in Spiritual Warfare

      II  Avoiding Works of the Flesh

      III  You are a chosen generation

The first thing I want to show you is how to use the word of God in waging spiritual warfare. I call it a Sword Drill. Let's do it like this:

1. First, I will tell you what an "Angel of Light" might say to tempt you.

2. Second, you let me know what kind of weapon they are using such as lies, pride, or gossip. We talked about these in Sex Lesson No. 4

3. Third, I will have you look up a scripture to meditate on when you are ignoring the temptation or that will use if the Holy Spirit tells you to use it.

(Fathers, I suggest you read the scripture after your son finds them in his Bible.)

# SWORD DRILL — WAGING SPIRITUAL WARFARE

| Angel of Light Says | Type of Weapon | Your Weapon<br>Hid in your heart | Comment |
|---|---|---|---|
| How can you handle a wife if you don't get some experience first? | Pride | **Titus 2:1-6**<br>*An aged man to teach me.* | Before and after you are married. |
| Look, you're supposed to have an education. How can you believe all that stuff? | Pride | **2 Corinthians 3:19**<br>*The wisdom of this world is foolishness with God.* | God told us the world was round when man said it was flat! |
| Look, if God didn't want you to do it, why did he give you sex organs anyway. | Lie | **Proverbs 5:18**<br>*Let thy fountain be blessed: and rejoice with the wife of thy youth.* | You will enjoy sex with your wife. |
| That's Old Testament stuff. It doesn't apply now. | Lie | **Romans 15:4**<br>*For whatsoever things were written aforetime were written for our learning...* | Religious lies are an abomination. |

| | | |
|---|---|---|
| I know some churches that don't believe that stuff. | Gossip | Make sure you never join any such "church"! |
| | | **Galatians 1:8** *But though we, or an angel from heaven, preach any other gospel unto you than that which we have preached unto you, **let him be accursed.*** |
| If you get some it will make you stronger. | Lie Pride | **I John 4:4** *Greater is he that is in me, than he that is in the world.* |
| If you don't make love to me, I'll always hate you. | Murder | **I John 3:15** *Whosoever hateth his brother is a murderer...* |
| Here I am, come to me. | Pride | **I Corinthians 6:18** *Flee fornication...* Joseph survived Potipher's wife with the strength of God's word. |
| I don't think you can abstain. | Pride | **Philippians 4:13** *I can do all things through Christ which strengtheneth me.* You may be unequally yoked |

*Sex Lesson #7*

# SWORD DRILL — WAGING SPIRITUAL WARFARE

| Angel of Light Says | Type of Weapon | Your Weapon Hid in your heart | Comment |
|---|---|---|---|
| Everybody is doing it but you. | Lie Pride | **Matthew 7:13** *...For wide is the gate, and broad is the way, that leadeth to destruction, and many there be which go in thereat.* | Besides, everybody is NOT doing it. |
| Get with it, man, can't you see the Church is dead. | Lie | **Matthew 16:18** *...Upon this rock I will build my Church; and the gates of hell shall not prevail against it.* | |
| If you don't do it, you will be all alone and a nobody. | Lie | **Hebrews 13:5** *...I will never leave thee, nor forsake thee. (Jesus)* | |

4

*Becoming More Like Jesus*

| | | | |
|---|---|---|---|
| Do you love me more than anything else in the world? | Pride | **Matthew 22:37** *...Love the Lord thy God with all thy heart...soul ...mind.* | |
| What are you afraid of? | Pride | **2 Timothy 1:7** *For God hath not given us the spirit of fear, but of power and of love, and of a sound mind.* | |
| A temptation that: Brings about confusion | Lie | **1 Corinthians 14:33** *For God is not the author of confusion, but of peace.* | If it's confusing, it's Satan. |
| A temptation that: Brings about Challenge or Embarrassment | Lie Pride | **Proverbs 16:18** *Pride goeth before destruction...* | |
| You are so strong, handsome and spiritual, can you help it? | Pride Flattery | **Proverbs 5:3-4** *3 For the lips of a strange woman drop as an honeycomb, and her mouth is smoother than oil* | Do not flatter. It is dangerous. |

5

*Sex Lesson #7*

## SWORD DRILL — WAGING SPIRITUAL WARFARE

| Angel of Light Says | Type of Weapon | Your Weapon Hid in your heart | Comment |
|---|---|---|---|
| | | 4 But her end is bitter as wormwood, sharp as a two-edged sword. | |
| You should be ashamed of all that stuff they teach you. | Lie | **Romans 1:16** For I am not ashamed of the gospel of Christ; for it is the power of God unto salvation to every one that believeth... | |
| It's not true. When is your Jesus coming back? | Lie Doubt | **2 Peter 3:9-10** 9 The Lord is not slack concerning his promise, as some men count slackness... 10 But the day of the Lord will come as the thief in the night... | |

6

| | | |
|---|---|---|
| It won't hurt you to go to the girlie joint. You won't have to do anything. | Lie | **2 Thessalonians 5:22** *Abstain from all appearance of evil.* You could be unequally yoked. |
| Look, that Bible was written by a bunch of hard up men. I'm telling you not to believe all that stuff. | Lie | **2 Timothy 3:16** *All scripture is given by inspiration of God...* |
| Their interpretation of what the Bible means is not right. | Lie | **2 Peter 1:20-21** *20 Knowing this first, that no prophecy of the scripture is of any **private interpretation.*** *21 For the prophecy came not in old time by the will of man: but holy men of God spake as they were moved by the Holy Ghost.* The Bible interprets itself. By comparing scripture with scripture, the deep truths and revelations come forth from the Holy Spirit himself. |

## Sex Lesson #7

# SWORD DRILL — WAGING SPIRITUAL WARFARE

| Angel of Light Says | Type of Weapon | Your Weapon Hid in your heart | Comment |
|---|---|---|---|
| You really won't die. Condoms will protect you from AIDS and all that other stuff. | Lie | **Romans 4:3** *...Let God be true, but every man a liar...* | Satan also told Eve she wouldn't die! |
| It will make you look more mature without acne and that squeaky voice. | Pride | **Ecclesiastes 12:8** *Vanity of vanities, saith the preacher; all is vanity.* | Sexual sinners continue to age fast. When they are 20 they look 30. When 40 they look 50. |
| Do it in this life, you can be good when you come back again. | Lie | **Hebrews 9:27** *And as it is appointed unto men once to die, but after this the judgment.* | There is no such thing as "reincarnation". |
| If it feels good, do it. | Pride | **Romans 12:1** *...that ye present your bodies a living sacrifice, holy, acceptable unto God, which is your reasonable service.* | |

## Becoming More Like Jesus

| | | |
|---|---|---|
| Don't believe all that stuff, your parents just don't want you to have fun the way they do. | Lie | **John 8:44**<br>*Ye are of your father the devil and the lusts of your father ye will do ...because there is no truth in him..for he is a liar, and the father of lies.* |
| A Very Clever Temptation | Lie<br>Pride | **Galatians 5:1**<br>*Stand fast in the liberty wherewith Christ has made us free, and not be entangled again in the yoke of bondage.* |
| I am going to rape you! | | *STOP, in the name of Jesus GET OUT, in the name of Jesus!* |

*Sex Lesson #7*

## II Avoiding Works of the Flesh

(The "works" are put in list form for your convenience.)

**Galatians 5:19**
*19 Now the works of the flesh are manifest, which are these;*
*Adultery*
**Fornication**
**Uncleanness**
**Lasciviousness**

**Galatians 5:20**
*Idolatry*
**Witchcraft**
*Hatred*
*Variance*
*Emulations*
*Wrath*
*Strife*
**Seditions**
*Heresies*

**Galatians 5:21**
*Envyings*
*Murders*
**Drunkenness**
**Revellings**
*And such like: of the which I tell you before, as I have also told you in time past, that they which do such things shall not inherit the kingdom of God.*

You can win the battle against sexual sin if you stay spiritually strong. However, Works of the Flesh such as those we will look at today open the door and invite sin in. So you should stay away from them.

(Following are comments on selected works of the flesh.)

**Adultery or Fornication**
**In a spiritual sense,** adultery or fornication is the giving of yourself to someone or something which is against your God.

10

**James 4:4**
*Ye adulterers and adulteresses, know ye not that the **friendship of the world is enmity with God?** Whosoever therefore will be a friend of the world is the enemy of God.*

**2 Corinthians 6:14**
*Be ye not unequally yoked together with unbelievers: For what fellowship hath righteousness with unrighteousness? And what communion hath light with darkness?*

In a young person's life, especially, this could include being unequally yoked with an unbeliever.

So this means that when you start to 'go steady', you should not be with an unbeliever.

This does allow you to have casual friendships with people though. It gives them a chance to see Jesus in you.

UNCLEANNESS
Masturbation is an uncleanness. Do not masturbate.

LASCIVIOUSNESS
Lasciviousness is a big word that means lust. It includes pornography. Do not be involved in any pornographic books, magazines, movies or television.

Sex Lesson #7

IDOLATRY

Worshipping any other god is idolatry. However hero worship, thing worship and state of being worship is also idolatry. I would like to be your role model. However, I am only a man and subject to failure. You should look to Jesus as your role model.

I want to warn you against trying to pattern your life after any man, no matter how successful that man might be.

Because if and when he fails, your world can fall apart. And their field could include any of the following: (Fathers, just select any that you think would be of interest to your son.)

| | | |
|---|---|---|
| o Musical Stars | o Business People | o Politicians |
| o World Leaders | o Doctors | o Lawyers |
| o Community Activists | o Preachers | o Teachers |
| o Pastors | o Scientists | o Inventor |
| o Elected Officials | o Sports Player | o Dancer |
| o Entertainer | o Fashion Model | |

In addition, do not worship any **institution, thing or state of being.**

| | | |
|---|---|---|
| o An education | o Top Ten List | o Hobby |
| o Social club | o Church organ. | o Recognition |
| o Self Esteem | o I Did It My Way | o Self Pride |
| o Self Respect | o Automobile | o House |
| o Article of Clothing | | o Church building |
| o Ministry for God | | o Stock/Financial Market |

WITCHCRAFT

The traditional view of a witch is a woman in a black dress stirring a pot over an open fire. The man involved in witchcraft was called a warlock. What they had in the pot was actually drugs. Today, instead of calling them witches and warlocks, they are called drug pushers and suppliers.

12

**The Greek words for witchcraft are:**

1. **Pharmakeia,** which means medication or pharmacy.

2. **Pharmakon,** which means a spell giving potion, a druggist, pharmacist or **poisoner.**

So when someone tries to sell or give you drugs, you treat them as a witch or warlock. Ignore them or tell them "No, in the name of Jesus."

**Romans 13:1**
*Let every soul be subject unto the higher powers. For there is no power but of God: the powers that be are ordained of God.*

And also,

**1 Samuel 15:23**
*For rebellion is as the sin of witchcraft, and stubbornness is as iniquity and idolatry. Because thou hast rejected the word of the LORD, he hath also rejected thee from being king.*

SEDITION
Sedition is the act of going against authority. You are to obey the authority that is put over you at home, at school and in the community. As it is written:

ENVYINGS
You are not to envy other Christians. Even in early days of the Church, some preached out of envy. As it is written:

## Sex Lesson #7

**Philippians 1:15-17**
*15 Some indeed preach Christ **even of envy** and strife; and some also of good will:*

*16 The one preach Christ of contention, not sincerely, supposing to add affliction to my bonds;*

*17 But the other of love, knowing that I am set for the defence of the gospel.*

**Proverbs 23:17**
*Let not thine heart envy sinners: but be thou in the fear (respect) of the LORD all the day long.*

Neither are you to envy sinners. Even though some of them may appear successful and happy on the outside they are suffering and on their way to hell. As it is written:

## DRUNKENNESS & REVELLINGS

You are not to be involved in alcohol or wild parties. They are often like a "halfway house" to sexual sin. The body is already weak. The alcohol makes it weaker. As it is written:

**2 Peter 4:3**
*For the time past of our life may suffice us to have wrought the will of the Gentiles (non-Jews), when we walked in lasciviousness, lusts, excess of wine, revellings, banquetings, and abominable idolatries.*

**Proverbs 31:6**
*Give strong drink unto him that is ready to perish, and wine unto those that be of heavy hearts.*

**Isaiah 5:22**
*Woe unto them that are mighty to drink wine, and men of strength to mingle strong drink.*

**1 Thessalonians 5:22**
*Abstain from all appearance of evil.*

## III You Are A Chosen Generation

**1 Peter 2:9**
*But ye are a chosen generation, a royal priesthood, an holy nation, a **peculiar people**...*

The word of God says you are a chosen generation. The world will think you peculiar.

God also called the Hebrews to be a peculiar people and a royal priesthood.

*Sex Lesson #7*

**Exodus 19:5-6**
*5 Now therefore, if ye will obey my voice indeed, and keep my covenant, then ye* **shall be a peculiar treasure unto me** *above all people: for all the earth is mine:*

*6 And ye shall be unto me a kingdom of priests, and an holy nation...*

**Genesis 12:1**
*Now the LORD had said unto Abram, "Get thee out of thy country, and from thy kindred, and from thy father's house, unto a land that I will shew thee:*

*2* **And I will** *make of thee a great nation, and I will bless thee, and* **make thy name great;** *and thou shalt be a blessing.*

*3 And I will bless them that bless thee, and curse him that curseth thee...*

God calls you out to be separate just as he called Abraham out of a sinful nation and people.

**Summary of Sex Lessons**

Son, the best way I can summarize these teachings is this:

1. God calls you to be separated from the world's values.
2. He wants to bless you.
3. **He** wants to make your name great.
   (Not **you** make your name great.)
4. God is not a man that he should lie. He delivers what he promises. (Titus 1:2)

## Scriptural References for Sex Lesson No. 7
(You may reproduce this list for your son or daughter)

**Sword Drill — Waging spiritual warfare.**
Tit 2:2 An aged man to teach me...
2 Cor 3:19 The wisdom of this world is foolishness to God.
Prov 5:18 fountain be blessed and rejoice with the wife of...
Rom 15:4 written aforetime were written for our learning.
Gal 1:8 preach any other gospel...let him be accursed.
1 Jn 4:4 Greater is he that is in me, than he that is ...
1 Jn 3:15 Whosoever hateth his brother is a murderer...
1 Cor 6:18 Flee fornication...
Rom 4:3 Let God be true, but every man a liar...
Eccl 12:8 Vanity of vanities...all is vanity.
Gal 5:1 Stand fast in the liberty...Christ hath made us free.
Heb 9:27 once to die, but after this the judgment.
Rom 12:1 present your bodies a living sacrifice.
Jn 8:44 For he is a liar, and the father of it.
Phil 4:13 do all things through Christ which strengtheneth me.
Mt 7:13 wide is the gate...that leadeth to destruction...
Mt 16:18 my Church...the gates of hell shall not prevail...
Heb 13:5 I will never leave thee, nor forsake thee.
Mt 22:37 Love God...heart...soul...mind...
Rom 8:31 If God be for us, who can be against us.
2 Tim 1:7 not given us the spirit of fear; but of power...
1 Cor 14:33 God is not the author of confusion, but of peace...
Prov 16:18 Pride goeth before destruction...
Prov 5:3 For the lips of a strange woman drop as an honeycomb.
Prov 5:4 But her end is bitter...sharp as a two-edged sword...
Rom 1:16 I am not ashamed of the gospel of Christ...
2 Pet 3:9 The Lord is not slack concerning his promise...
2 Pet 3:10 the day of the Lord will come as a thief in the night.
2 Thes 5:22 Abstain from all appearance of evil.
2 Tim 3:16 All scripture is given by inspiration of God...
2 Pet 1:20 no scripture is of any private interpretation.
2 Pet 1:21 Prophecy came not...by will of man...but of God.

*Sex Lesson #7*

**Avoiding Works of the Flesh**
Gal 5:19 works of the flesh are these...adultery, fornication...
Gal 5:20 idolatry, witchcraft... seditions...
Gal 5:21 drunkenness, revellings... not inherit the kingdom...
Jas 4:4 Ye adulterers and adulteresses...the enemy of God.
2 Cor 6:14 Be ye not unequally yoked together with unbelievers...
Rom 13:1 every soul be subject unto the higher powers...
1 Sam 15:23 Rebellion is as the sin of witchcraft...
Phil 1:15 Some indeed preach Christ even of envy and strife...
Phil 1:16 not sincerely, supposing to add affliction...
Phil 1:17 Knowing that I am set for the defence of the gospel...
Prov 23:17 Let not thine heart envy sinners...
2 Pet 4:3 we walked in lasciviousness, lusts, excess of wine...
Prov 31:6 strong drink unto him that is ready to perish...
Isa 5:22 Woe unto them that are mighty to drink wine...
1 Thes 5:22 Abstain from all appearance of evil.

**You are a chosen generation.**
1 Pet 2:9 a royal priesthood... chosen...a peculiar people...
Exo 19:5 ye shall be a peculiar treasure unto me...
Exo 19:6 ye shall be unto me a kingdom of priests...
Gen 12:1 Get thee out of thy country...
Gen 12:2 will make of thee a great nation...thy name great...
Gen 12:3 will bless them that bless thee...curse him that...

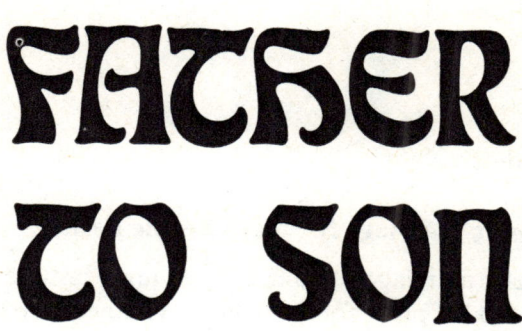

# FATHER TO SON

## Volume III

### Counseling For Pre-Marriage

Author's Note

**If your Marriage Hasn't Been The Best...**

Every marriage should be a living example of God's plan for marriage. Chances are however, such is not the case in many families.

But that is no reason to sit and do nothing for your children. God gives us a calling to teach them, even though we are not perfect ourselves. He simply tells us to do it.

Besides, as we see the glory of God's light, we can move our own marriages toward his plan for marriage. And as we do this, we can then become both the message as well as the messenger to our children.

And since some young people think they will be better at marriage and parenting than we are, we will be giving them the best plan to go by when we teach them God's plan.

*Overview*
*Pre-Marriage Lesson No. 1*

# *Marriage Is Ordained By God*

The whole idea of marriage came from God. He said that man should not be alone. This first teaching is on the marriage institution. We will be covering several very important points:

    I  God ordains marriage

   II  Marriage is permanent

  III  One flesh has special meaning

  IV  God will give you a wife

    V  You should marry another Christian

  VI  You should not be a bachelor on your own

 VII  Relatives or friends should not stay with you

However, you do not have to marry if you have the gift of celibacy and want to give your life wholly to God. (I Corinthians 7)

*Pre-Marriage Lesson #1*

## How to Introduce The Lessons On Pre Marriage

(As an introduction of the subject of marriage, I suggest you read the following scriptures to your son.)

Let me read some scriptures from Genesis to show how God ordained marriage. Then we will get into the details of what this means.

### Genesis 2:18-25

*18 And the LORD God said,* **"It is not good that the man should be alone; I will make him an help meet for him."**

*19 And out of the ground the LORD God formed every beast of the field, and every fowl of the air; and brought them unto Adam to see what he would call them: and whatsoever Adam called every living creature, that was the name thereof.*

*20 And Adam gave names to all cattle, and to the fowls of the air, but for Adam there was not found an help meet for him.*

*21 And the LORD God caused a deep sleep to fall upon Adam and he slept: and he took one of his ribs, and closed up the flesh instead thereof;*

*22 And the rib, which the LORD God had taken from man, made he a woman, and brought her unto the man.*

*23 And Adam said, "This is* **now bone of my bones, and flesh of my flesh:** *she shall be called Woman, because she was taken out of Man."*

*24* **Therefore shall a man leave his father and his mother, and shall cleave unto his wife: and they shall be one flesh.**

*25 And they were both naked, the man and his wife, and were not ashamed.*

**Notes:**

*Marriage Is Ordained By God*

## I Does God Ordain Marriage?  Yes

Genesis 2:24 makes it very clear that God ordains marriage. Also, read Hebrews 13:4. It says marriage is honourable.

**Hebrews 13:4**
*Marriage is honourable in all, and the bed undefiled: but whore mongers and adulterers God will judge.*

## II Is Marriage Permanent?  Yes

Matthew 19:6 makes it clear.

**Matthew 19:6**
*Wherefore they are no more twain, but one flesh. What therefore God hath joined together, let no man put asunder.*

You and your wife become one flesh when you get married.

## III 'One Flesh' Has Special Meaning in Marriage

**Genesis 2:21**
*And the LORD God caused a deep sleep to fall upon Adam, and he slept: and he took one of his ribs, and closed up the flesh instead thereof.*

(Have your son read all of the scriptures before making these comments.)

**Genesis 2:23-24**
*23 And Adam said, "This is now bone of my bones, and*

## Pre-Marriage Lesson #1

*flesh of my flesh: she shall be called Woman, because she was taken out of Man."*

*24 Therefore shall a man leave his father and his mother and shall cleave unto his wife and they shall be "one flesh."*

Not only does One Flesh mean to walk together, they also mean the words I, MY, MINE and YOURS virtually leave your vocabulary and your wife's.

They are replaced by words like WE, OUR and THE. This applies to money, checking and savings accounts, automobiles, furniture, children and everything except the most personal items exclusive to a husband or wife.

The following kinds of items become OUR or THE:

- Money
- Car (Or the blue car)
- Stereo
- Bill
- Loan
- Son
- Daughter
- Problem
- Family Bible
- House
- Etc.

The following kinds of items remain YOURS or MINE:

- Toothbrush
- Bible

*Marriage Is Ordained By God*

- Watch
- Underwear
- Dress
- Etc.

## IV  Will God Give Me a Wife?                              Yes

**Genesis 2:22**
*And the rib, which the LORD God had taken from man, made he a woman, and brought her unto the man.*

As God gave a wife to Adam he will give a wife to you.

**Proverbs 18:22**
*Whoso findeth a wife findeth a good thing, and obtaineth favour of the LORD.*

A wife is a favor from God.

**Proverbs 19:14**
*House and riches are the inheritance of fathers: and a prudent wife is from the LORD.*

A wise wife comes from God.

## V  Should Christians Marry Non-Christians                  No

To marry a Non Christian you would be unequally yoked. Would you read 2 Corinthians 6:14?

**2 Corinthians 6:14**
*Be ye not unequally yoked together with unbelievers: For what fellowship hath righteousness with unrighteousness? And what communion hath light with darkness?*

Being yoked with unbelievers was the trigger to Solomon's downfall. (2 Samuel 11:1-9)

*Pre-Marriage Lesson #1*

## VI. Should I Be A Bachelor On My Own First?   No

Would You re-read verses 24 and 18 of Genesis chapter 2. I think you will see it there.

**Genesis 2:24**
*Therefore shall a man leave his father and his mother and shall cleave unto his wife: and they shall be one flesh.*

**Genesis 2:18**
*And the LORD God said, "It is not good that the man should be alone; I will make him an help meet for him."*

The key words here are **"leave and cleave"** and **"not good that the man should be alone."**

If you or your wife-to-be lived away from your parents you would be more susceptible to sexual sin.

Satan could steal the blood covenant sealing of your marriage.

## VII. Should Our Relatives Stay With Us? Us With Them?   No

Here again, the word says 'leave and cleave.' It does not say 'leave and take.'

*Marriage Is Ordained By God*

### Scriptural References for Pre-Marriage Lesson No. 1
(This list may be reproduced for your son or daughter.)

**Introducing the Lessons on Marriage**
Gen 2:18 not good that the man should be alone...an help meet...
Gen 2:19 to see what he would call them; and whatsoever Adam...
Gen 2:20 but for Adam there was not found an help meet for him...
Gen 2:21 and he took one of his ribs, and closed up the flesh...
Gen 2:22 made he a woman, and brought her unto the man...
Gen 2:23 now bone of my bones, and flesh of my flesh...
Gen 2:24 leave his father and his mother...cleave unto his wife...
Gen 2:25 the man and his wife, and were not ashamed.

**God Ordains Marriage**
Heb 13:4 Marriage is honourable...adulterers God will judge.

**Marriage is permanent**
Mt 19:6 God hath joined together, let no man put asunder.

**One Flesh has special meaning**
Gen 2:21 deep sleep to fall upon Adam...took one of his ribs...
Gen 2:23 now bone of my bones, and flesh of my flesh...
Gen 2:24 cleave unto his wife and they shall be one flesh.

**God will give you a wife**
Gen 2:22 and brought her unto the man.
Prov 18:22 findeth a good thing...favour of the LORD.
Prov 19:14 and a prudent wife is from the LORD.

**Christians should only marry other Christians**
2 Cor 6:14 Be ye not unequally yoked together with unbelievers...

**You should not be a bachelor living alone**
Gen 2:24 Therefore shall a man leave...and cleave unto his wife...
Gen 2:18 It is not good that the man should be alone...

**Relatives should not stay with you**
Gen 2:24 Therefore shall a man leave...and cleave unto his wife...

*Overview*
*Pre-Marriage Lesson No. 2*

# Duties of the Husband and Wife

---

We have already talked about the marriage institution being ordained by God. Today we will talk about your responsibilities as the husband.

We will also talk about your fiancee's responsibilities as a wife. Let me give you a quick review of what the scriptures say:

    I  The three ways you should love your wife

    II  Your leadership responsibility

    III  Your responsibility to provide for your family

    IV  The dangers of not honoring your wife

    V  The three ways your wife should love you

    VI  Your wife's responsibility for the household

*Pre-Marriage Lesson #2*

## How Many Ways Should I Love My Wife?  Three (3)

You should love your wife with the three kinds of love that we talked about in the Sex Lesson No. 1:

1. Agape love. (God's Love)
2. Phileo love. (Friendship)
3. Erotic love. (Sexual)

Let's look at an Agape Love Scripture first.

**Ephesians 5:25**
*Husbands, love your wives, even as Christ also loved the church, and gave himself for it.*

This means you should give yourself for your wife.

(Allow time for discussion at this point. Also, the 13th chapter of 1 Corinthians is an excellent chapter on love.)

Now let's look at Phileo love.

**Ephesians 5:28-29**
*28 So ought men to love their wives as their own bodies. He that loveth his wife loveth himself.*

*29 For no man ever yet hated his own flesh; but nourisheth and cherisheth it, even as the Lord the church:*

Son, you are to love your wife as you love yourself.

**Colossians 3:19**
*Husbands, love your wives, and be not bitter against them.*

Now, let's look at Erotic Love.

**Ephesians 5:21**
*Submitting yourselves one to another in fear of God.*

You and your wife are to submit sexually to each other. We will be talking more about sex in Marriage Lesson No. 3.

## II  Who Should Be the Head of the Marriage?°  — Husband

You are the head of the marriage, son. Let's look at some scriptures on this.

**1 Corinthians 11:3, 8-9**
*3 But I would have you know, that the head of every man is Christ; and the head of the woman is the man; and the head of Christ is God.*

*8 For the man is not of the woman; but the woman of the man.*

As Christ is the head of the church, you are the head of your wife. She was created for you.

*9 Neither was the man created for the woman; but the woman for the man.*

**Genesis 2:21**
*And the LORD God caused a deep sleep to fall upon Adam, and he slept: and he took one of his ribs, and closed up the flesh instead thereof:*

Your wife is to be at your side, not under your feet and not a competitor. The rib comes out of the side. You are to love her as you love yourself.

*Pre-Marriage Lesson #2*

## III  Is The Husband to Provide for His Wife & Family?     Yes

You are responsible to provide for your wife and children. Would you read the scripture that says this in Timothy?

**1 Timothy 5:8**
*But if any provide not for his own, and specially for those of his own house, he hath denied the faith, and is worse than an infidel.*

If you don't provide for your own household, God sees you as worse than someone who has denied Jesus.

## III  Can I Suffer If I Don't Honor My Wife?     Yes

Read the following scripture from Peter and you'll see what happens if you do not honor your wife.

**1 Peter 3:8**
*Likewise, ye husbands, dwell with them **according to knowledge**, giving honour unto the weaker vessel, and as being heirs together of the grace of life; **that your prayers be not hindered**.*

There are two things I want to show you in this scripture:
1. You must have the 'knowledge' necessary to lead your wife.

2. If you mistreat your wife, your prayers may not get answered.

## V How Many Ways Should My Wife Love Me?    Three (3)

**Ephesians 5:22-23**
*22 Wives, submit yourselves unto your own husbands, as unto the Lord.*

*23 For the husband is the head of the wife, even as Christ is the head of the church: and he is the saviour of the body.*

**Ephesians 5:33** *(partial)*
*And the wife see that she reverence her husband.*

Your wife should love you with the Agape Love of God, the Phileo Love of Friendship and the Erotic Love of Sex.

Your wife's Agape love for you should be like her love for Christ.

She should submit to your will.

She should be your **best friend.**

(Submission does not mean dictatorial domination).

## VI Who Is Responsible For the House?    The Wife

**Titus 2:5**
*To be discreet, chaste, keepers at home, good, obedient to their own husbands, that the word of God be not blasphemed."*

**Proverbs 31: (various verses)**
*10 Who can find a virtuous woman? For her price (worth) is far above rubies.*

*13 She seeketh wool, and flax and worketh willingly with her hands.*

Your wife is responsible for keeping the household as outlined in these scriptures.

God says a woman who does his will and that of her husband is priceless.

She shops for clothing and goods.

*Pre-Marriage Lesson #2*

*14 She is like the merchants ships; she bringeth her food from afar.*

She shops for foods, including foods from afar (exotic foods).

*15 She riseth also while it is yet night, and giveth meat to her household, and a portion to her maidens.*

She attends to the needs of her house, including her servants.

*22 She maketh herself coverings of tapestry; her clothing is silk and purple.*

She dresses in fine clothing (appealing to her husband).

*27 She looketh well to the ways of her household, and eateth not the bread of idleness.*

She does not just sit around idle.

*28 Her children arise up, and call her blessed: her husband also, and he praiseth her.*

Her children cherish her.

Her husband praises her (not criticizes her).

*30 Favour is deceitful, and beauty is vain: but a woman that feareth the LORD, she shall be praised.*

Your wife is to respect you as she respects God.

**Closing Comments**

The benefits of doing it God's way include:

- Children get the love and attention they want and need.
- Children are supervised making it more difficult for them to get pregnant.
- Your wife works to glorify God through you and your children, **not** supervisors, employees, customers, students, clients, patients or etc.

*Duties of the Husband & Wife*

**Scriptural References for Marriage Lesson No. 2**
(You may reproduce this list for your son or daughter)

**You should love your wife three ways**
Eph 5:25 love your wives, even as Christ also loved the church...
Eph 5:28 So ought men to love their wives as their own bodies...
Eph 5:29 For no man ever yet hated his own flesh...
Col 3:19 Husbands, love your wives...be not bitter against them.
Eph 5:21 Submitting yourselves one to another in the fear of God.

**The man is the head of the marriage**
1 Cor 11:3 head of every man is Christ...of the woman is the man...
1 Cor 11:8 man is not of the woman, but the woman of the man.
1 Cor 11:9 Neither was the man created for the woman; but the...
Gen 2:21 and he took one of his ribs...

**The man is to provide**
1 Tim 5:8 if any not provide...is worse than an infidel.

**Man can be penalized for not honoring his wife**
1 Pet 3:8 honour unto the weaker vessel...prayers not be hindered...

**Your wife should love you three ways**
Eph 5:22 submit yourselves unto your own husbands, as unto...
Eph 5:23 husband is head of the wife, even as Christ is head...
Eph 5:33 And the wife see that she reverence her husband.

**Your wife is responsible for the house**
Tit 2:5 to be discreet chaste, keepers at home...
Prov 31:10 a virtuous woman? ...is far above rubies...
Prov 31:13 worketh willingly with her hands.
Prov 31:14 she bringeth her food from afar.
Prov 31:15 is yet night...meat to her household...maidens...
Prov 31:22 coverings of tapestry...silk and purple.
Prov 31:27 looketh well to the ways of her household...
Prov 31:28 call her blessed...husband..praiseth her...
Prov 31:30 a woman that feareth the LORD, she shall be praised.

*Overview*
*Pre-Marriage Lesson No. 3*

# Sexual Relations

We have talked about your responsibility to love your wife and your wife's responsibility to love you.

Today, we are going to talk more about what the scriptures have to say about sex. We will be making several points:

- I God wants you and your wife to enjoy sex with each other.
- II I will teach you how to love your wife sexually.
- III God describes his agape love relationship with man as man would describe sexual love with a woman.
  **Special Note:**
  You may want to delay teaching this section until your teenager is close to getting married.
- IV Sex is for having children.
- V You should not have sex during your wife's menstrual.
- VI You should not have sex with your wife before marriage.
- VII You should not commit sexual sins.

*Pre-Marriage Lesson #3*

---

VIII  You should not buy sex.

IX  You should not commit adultery.

X  Abstinence has conditions.

XI  Your spouse has authority over your body.

### I Does God Want You and Your Wife to Enjoy Sex?    Yes

There is no question about it, son. God wants you to enjoy sex. Read this passage from Proverbs:

**Proverbs 5:18-19**
*18 Let thy fountain be blessed: and rejoice with the wife of thy youth.*

*19 Let her be as the loving hind and pleasant roe; let her breasts satisfy thee at all times and be thou ravished always with her love.*

Let me define these words to make sure you understand you are to enjoy sex with your wife.

- 'Fountain' refers to your sex organ.

- 'Rejoice' means to be made very happy.

- 'Loving' means tender affection.

- You are to enjoy her 'breasts.'

- 'Satisfy' means abundantly satisfied, not just contentment.

## Sexual Relations

- 'Ravished' means you are to be caught up by her lovemaking — actually enraptured or intoxicated by it.

- A 'hind' is a sure footed deer that clings to the sides of steep mountains as it climbs.

- A 'roe' is a specie of deer that are monogamous. They only have one mate.

### II Should Someone Teach You How to Love Sexually?   Yes

As your father, I will teach you how to love your wife sexually.

And either your wife's mother (or some older, discreet woman should teach your wife how to love you sexually.

**Titus 2:1-6**
*1 But speak thou the things which become sound doctrine:*

*2 That the aged men be **sober, grave, temperate, sound in faith, in charity, in patience.***

*3 The aged women likewise, that they be in behaviour as becometh **holiness, not false accusers, not given to much wine, teachers of good things;***

Both the aged man and aged woman must be sound in the Christian faith. And they must not gossip. Teaching young people about sexual intercourse is very private.

*Pre-Marriage Lesson #3*

*4 That they may teach young women to be sober, to love their husbands, to love their children.*

*5 To be discreet, chaste, keepers at home, good, obedient to their own husbands, that the word of God not be blasphemed.*

*6 Young men likewise exhort to be sober minded.*

(See caution about selection of the **aged** man or woman in Sex Lesson No. 1)

### III  Does God Describe Sexual Love?    Yes

God is a spirit and identifies with man. Though man is a spirit, he more readily identifies with flesh.

Therefore, in the Song of Solomon, God uses man's understanding of erotic love to tell us that he loves (agape) us as we love (etheleo) to love (erotic).

Sexual love involves more than just sexual intercourse. It includes:

Kissing & Talking, Caressing Pleasant Aromas, Fine Bodies

Notes:
_____
_____

## Sexual Relations

### Kissing & Talking

**Song of Solomon 7:9**
*And the roof of thy mouth like the best wine for my beloved, that goeth down sweetly, causing the lips of those that are asleep to speak.*

Intimate kissing and talking should be done before, during and after sexual intercourse.

**Song of Solomon 2:8** *The voice of my beloved! Behold, he cometh leaping upon the mountains, skipping upon the hills.*

Communication is unrestrained after intercourse, just as prayer is unrestrained after praise.

### Caressing the Body

**Song of Solomon 8:1,3**
*1 O that thou wert as my brother, that sucked the breasts of my mother! When I should find thee without, I would kiss thee; yea, I should not be despised.*

The breasts are a sensitive point of stimulation before, during and after intercourse.

*3 His left hand should be under my head, and his right hand should embrace me.*

The hands should also be used to hold and embrace your spouse. And she to embrace you.

Notes:
_____
_____
_____

*Pre-Marriage Lesson #3*

## Pleasant Aromas

Your bodies (including your breath) should be clean, refreshed and anointed with aromas pleasing to each other.

**Song of Solomon 4:11**
*Thy lips, O my spouse, drop as the honeycomb: Honey and milk are under thy tongue; and the smell of thy garments is like the smell of Lebanon.*

**Song of Solomon 1:13**
*A bundle of myrrh is my well-beloved unto me; he shall lie all night betwixt my breasts.*

**Song of Solomon 5:13**
*His cheeks are as a bed of spices, as sweet flowers; his lips, like lilies, dropping sweet smelling myrrh.*

After sexual intercourse, your bodies should be cleaned and refreshed as soon as reasonable.

## Fine Bodies

Both you and your wife should keep your bodies in the best of shape for each other.

**Song of Solomon 5:15**
*His legs are as pillars of marble, set upon sockets of fine gold: His countenance is as Lebanon, excellent as the cedars.*

## Sexual Relations

**Song of Solomon 7:6-7**
*6 How fair and how pleasant art thou, O love, for delights!*

*7 This thy stature is like to a palm tree, and thy breasts to clusters of grapes.*

**Song of Solomon 7:10**
*I am my beloved's, and his desire is toward me.*

Your appearance to each other is to be superb and you should desire each other, but in second place to your desire for God.

### IV  Is Sex Intended For Having Children?  Yes

**Genesis 1:27-28**
*27 So God created man in his own image, in the image of God created he him; male and female created he them.*

*28 And God blessed them and God said unto them, 'Be fruitful, and multiply, and replenish the earth..."*

### V  Should We Have Sex During Her Menstrual?  No

**Leviticus 16:24**
*And if any man lie with her at all, and her flowers be upon him, he shall be unclean seven days; and all the bed whereon he lieth shall be unclean.*

When the scripture says flower here, it is referring to your wife's menstrual period.

Don't have sex during this period.

*Pre-Marriage Lesson #3*

## VI  Should We Try Each Other Out Before We Marry?   No

To do that would be the sin of Fornication. We talked about that in Sex Lesson No. 2.

**1 Corinthians 7:2**
*Nevertheless, to avoid fornication, let every man have his own wife, and let every woman have her own husband.*

## VII  Can We Have Oral or Anal Sex or Masturbate After We Are Married?   No

All sexual sins, including masturbation, oral sex and anal sex are Sin no matter if you are a child, adult, married or single.

## VIII  Can I Buy Sex Sometimes?   No

To join your body, the temple of God's Holy Spirit, to a prostitute is Sin.

**1 Corinthians 6:15**
*Know ye not that your bodies are the members of Christ? Shall I then take the members of Christ, and make them the members of an harlot? God forbid.*

It doesn't matter if your wife is pregnant, sick, out of town or whatever. You are not to have a prostitute.

*Sexual Relations*

### IX Can I Have Some Other Woman Sometimes?    No

**Exodus 20:14**
*Thou shalt not commit adultery.*

The scriptures are clear. Adultery is sin.

### X Should My Wife and I Ever Abstain From Sex?    Yes, If...

**1 Corinthians 7:5**
*Defraud ye not one the other, except it be with consent for a time, that ye may give yourselves to fasting and prayer; and come together again, that Satan tempt you not for your incontinency."*

But only according to the following scripture.

Remember. Even when you stop having sex for prayer and fasting, it must be with your consent as head of the house.

### XI Should the Husband or Wife Initiate Sex?    Either!

Either you or your wife. Your bodies do not belong to yourselves. They belong to each other.

**1 Corinthians 7:3-4**
*3 Let the husband render unto the wife due benevolence: and likewise also the wife unto the husband.*

*4 The wife hath not power of her own body, but the husband: and likewise also the husband hath not power of his own body, but the wife.*

Sex should not be withheld from each other. It can be planned or impromtu.

(In this scripture,'power' means authority.)

*Pre-Marriage Lesson #3*

## Scriptural References for Pre-Marriage Lesson No. 3
(You may copy this list for your son or daughter)

**God want you and your wife to enjoy sex**
Prov 5:18 thy fountain be blessed...with the wife of thy youth.
Prov 5:19 her breasts satisfy thee at all times...ravished with...

**Someone should teach you how to love sexually**
Tit 2:1 Speak thou the things which become sound doctrine.
Tit 2:2 aged men be sober, grave, temperate, sound in faith...
Tit 2:3 aged women likewise ...teachers of good things...
Tit 2:4 may teach the young women to...love their husbands...
Tit 2:5 To be ...obedient to their own husbands, that the word...
Tit 2:6 Young men likewise exhort to be sober minded...

**God describes sexual love**
Song 7:9 roof of thy mouth like the best wine for my beloved...
Song 2:8 voice of my beloved...upon the mountains...the hills...
Song 8:1 that sucked the breasts of my mother...not be despised.
Song 8:3 left hand should be under my head...should embrace me...
Song 4:11 and the smell of thy garments is like the smell of...
Song 1:13 bundle of myrrh is my beloved unto me...betwixt my...
Song 5:13 his lips, like lilies, dropping sweet smelling myrrh...
Song 5:15 legs are as pillars of marble, set upon sockets of...
Song 7:6 how pleasant art thou, O love, for delights!
Song 7:7 to a palm tree, and thy breasts to clusters of grapes.
Song 7:10 I am my beloved's, and his desire is toward me.

**Sex is for procreating the species**
Gen 1:27 created man in his own image, in the image of God...
Gen 1:28 Be fruitful, and multiply, and replenish the earth...

**You should not have sex during her menstrual**
Lev 16:24 lie with her...her flowers be upon him, he shall be...

**You should not have sex with her before marriage**
1 Cor 7:2 to avoid fornication, let every man have his own wife.

**You should not have sex with a prostitute for any reason**
1 Cor 6:15 them the members of an harlot? God forbid.

**You should not have sex with anyone but your wife**
Exo 20:14 Thou shalt not commit adultery.

**You and you wife should not withhold sex from each other**
1 Cor 7:5 Defraud ye not, except it be with consent...

**Your body belongs to your wife, her body to you**
1 Cor 7:3 husband render...due benevolence...also the wife...
1 Cor 7:4 wife not power of her own body, but the husband...

*Overview*
*Pre-Marriage Lesson No. 4*

# Duties of Parents & Children

Today we are going to talk about your responsibility as a father and your wife's responsibility as a mother.

And though your wife will spend more time in parenting since she is the keeper of the house, you are still responsible for the job she does.

That is a part of your being the head of the wife as Christ is the head of the Church.

Your responsibilities as parents are:
- I  To love your children
- II  To teach your children
- III  To train your children
- IV  To chastise your children when necessary
- V  To use the rod on your children when necessary
- VI  Not to provoke your children to anger
- VII  To Honor your children

Your children's responsibilities are:
- VIII  To honor & obey their father and mother.

*Pre-Marriage Lesson #4*

## I To Love Your Children

**Titus 2:4**
*That they may teach the young women to be sober, to love their husbands, **to love their children.***

**Titus 2:6**
*Young men likewise...*

You love them with the Agape love of God and the Philoteknos love of parents for children. (See Sex Lesson No. 1)

Love of children requires:

- Time and attention to their needs.

- Teaching them the love of God.

- Training them in the ways of the Lord — obedience to Him and their parents.

- Chastising them when necessary.

- Not provoking them to anger.

## II To Teach Your Children The Word of God

**Deuteronomy 6:6-8**
*6 And these words, which I command thee this day, shall be in thine heart:*

*7 And thou shalt teach them diligently unto thy children, and shalt talk of them when thou sittest in thine house, and*

The scriptures in Deuteronomy say it well.

*when thou walkest by the way, and when thou liest down, and when thou risest up.*

*8 And thou shalt bind them for a sign upon thine hand, and they shall be as frontlets between thine eyes.*

*9 And thou shalt write them upon the posts of thy house, and on thy gates.*

These scriptures say that you should teach them the word of God all the time.

## III To Train Your Children

**Proverbs 22:6**
*Train up a child in the way he should go: and when he is old, he will not depart from it.*

### Teaching And Training Are Different

To teach your children is to make something known to them.

To train your children is to make sure they do what you have taught them.

For example, I taught you to brush your teeth one or two times. But I trained you to brush your teeth by constantly reminding to brush them until it became habit.

You must both teach and train your children.

*Pre-Marriage Lesson #4*

## IV To Chastise Your Children

**Hebrews 12:8**
*But if ye be without chastisement, whereof all are partakers, then are ye bastards, and not sons.*

To chastise means to correct.

What God is saying is if you love your children, you will chastise them.

If you don't chastise them, they may as well be bastards.

## V To Use the Rod When Necessary

**Proverbs 22:15**
*Foolishness is bound in the heart of a child: but the rod of correction shall drive it far from him.*

Use the rod when they continue to act foolishly.

**Proverbs 23:13-14**
*13 Withhold not correction from the child: for if thou beatest him with the rod, he shall not die.*

They won't die.

*14 Thou shalt beat him with the rod, and shalt deliver his soul from hell.*

It will save them from all kinds of trouble.

**Proverbs 13:24**
*He that spareth his rod hateth his son: but he that loveth him chasteneth him betimes.*

If you don't chastise your children, you hate them.

"Betimes" means early. It is easier to correct them while they are young than trying when they are older.

## VI NOT To Provoke Your Children to Anger

**Ephesians 6:4**
*And, ye fathers, provoke not your children to wrath: but bring them up in the nurture and admonition of the Lord.*

**Colossians 3:21**
*Fathers, provoke not your children to anger, lest they be discouraged.*

God is saying that we must not chastise our children to the point of anger.

(In addition, you should never chastise children while you are angry.)

## VII Parents To Honor Their Children

**Proverbs 20:7**
*The just man walketh in his integrity: His children are blessed after him*

**Proverbs 17:6**
*Children's children are the crown of old men; and **the glory of children are their fathers.***

Your children look at their father as God's man. They are blessed as you live up to God's word.

You should not let your child down. As you live the life of faith, you remain their glory. You must live the life you teach them.

## VIII Children To Honor & Obey Their Parents

**Ephesians 6:1-3**
*1 Children, obey your parents in the Lord: For this is right.*

*2 Honour thy father and mother; which is the first commandment with promise.*

God says it is right for children to obey their parents.

*Pre-Marriage Lesson #4*

*3 That it may be well with thee, and thou mayest live long on the earth.*

**Colossians 3:20**
*Children, obey your parents in all things: For this is well pleasing unto the Lord.*

God promises long life for children who honor their parents.

Children are to obey in all things including:

- Bedtime
- Curfews
- Baby sitters
- Television Privileges
- Clean rooms
- Behavior
- School work

## Scriptural References for Pre-Marriage Lesson No. 4
(You may reproduce this list for your son or daughter.)

**To love your children**
Tit 2:4 the young women to ... love their children.
Tit 2:6 Young men likewise...

**To teach your children the word of God**
Deut 6:6 And these words, which I command thee this day...
Deut 6:7 thou shalt teach them diligently unto thy children...
Deut 6:8 thou shalt bind them for a sign upon thine hand...
Deut 6:9 thou shalt write them upon the posts of thy house...

**To train your children**
Prov 22:6 Train up a child in the way he should go...

**To chastise your children**
Heb 12:8 without chastisement...then are ye bastards, not sons.

**To use the rod when necessary**
Prov 22:15 Foolishness is bound in the heart of a child, but...
Prov 23:13 If thou beatest him with the rod, he shall not die...
Prov 23:14 with the rod, and shalt deliver his soul from hell...
Prov 13:24 He that spareth his rod, hateth his son: but he...

**Not to provoke your children to anger**
Eph 6:4 provoke not your children to wrath: but bring them up...
Col 3:21 not your children to anger, lest they be discouraged...

**Parents to honor their children**
Prov 20:7 walketh in his integrity: His children are blessed...
Prov 17:6 the glory of children are their fathers...

**Children to honor and obey their parents**
Eph 6:1 Children, obey your parents in the Lord, for it is right.
Eph 6:2 Honour thy father and mother; which is the first ...
Eph 6:3 That it may be well with thee, and thou mayest live long...
Col 3:20 your parents...For this is well pleasing unto the Lord.

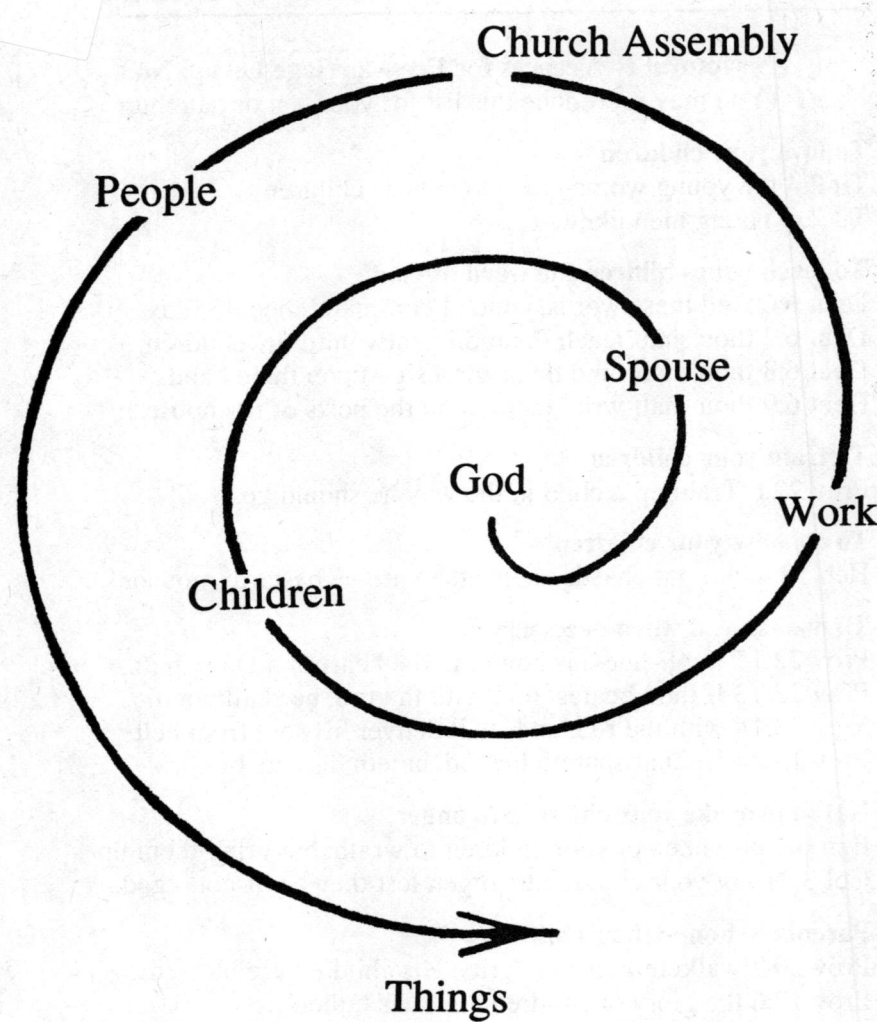

**SCRIPTURAL PRIORITIES**
An illustration
The priorities of life should
be centered around God.

*Overview*
*Pre-Marriage Lesson No. 5*

# Priorities & Problem Prevention

No matter how much you and your wife love each other, you will have problems in your marriage relationship.

One of the ways to keep these situations from boiling over is to know and act on the priorities God establishes in his word. Using God's priorities can help prevent many of the problems you will have in life.

Although the Bible does not give us an exact list, a study of the scriptures reveals the following priorities:

    I  God is first.
   II  Your wife is second.
  III  Your children are third.
  IV  Your work is fourth.
   V  Church assembly is fifth.
  VI  Husband's family before the wife's family.
 VII  Christians before non-Christians.
VIII  Things are last.

*Pre-Marriage Lesson #5*

I want you to know that this list is not a straight line with God at the top and things at the bottom.

Instead, it is a spiral list with God at the center and things on the perimeter. This sketch shows it pretty well. (Show sketch opposite page 1 of this lesson.)

Without question, however, prayer is the most ideal way to make decisions when you don't find specific answers in the word of God.

## 1 God is 1st

**Matthew 6:31-33**
*31 Therefore take no thought, saying:*
*'What shall we eat?' Or,*
*'What shall we drink?' Or,*
*'Wherewithal shall we be clothed?'*

*32 (For after all these things do the Gentiles seek:) for your heavenly Father knoweth that ye have need of all these things.*

*33 But seek ye first the kingdom of God, and his righteousness; and all these things shall be added unto you.*

Do The Scriptures Say How To Make God No. 1?

God is saying to put Him first. Then all the things of life will be added. (In the current times this includes higher education, automobiles, houses, recreation and etc.)

(Yes. See Pre-Marriage Lesson No. 6 for details if not already covered.)

Notes:

*Priorities & Problem Prevention*

## II Your Wife is 2nd

**Ephesians 5:23**
*For the husband is the head of the wife, even as Christ is the head of the church: and he is the saviour of the body.*

As God, in the person of Christ, is first to the husband, your wife is second to God in your life.

**Ephesians 5:28 (partial)**
*He that loveth his wife loveth himself.*

She is bone of your bone and flesh of your flesh.

There should always be time for her as the second priority in your life.

## III Your Children are 3rd

**1 Timothy 3:4-5**
*4 One that ruleth well his own house, having his children in subjection with all gravity;*

*5 For if a man know not how to rule his own house, how shall he take care of the church of God?*

Your children are from your flesh. Their seed was in your body. When you love your children, you love yourself.

Notes:
_____
_____
_____
_____
_____
_____
_____

*Pre-Marriage Lesson #5*

## IV. Work is 4th

There are two types of work.

1. One is the labor to provide for your family.
2. The other is work in the Church.

**Ephesians 4:1,11**
*1 I therefore, the prisoner of the Lord, beseech you that ye walk worthy of the vocation wherewith ye are called.*

*11 And he gave some, **apostles; and some, prophets; and some, evangelists; and some, pastors and teachers.***

**MINISTRY OFFICE**
If God has called you to a vocation of one of the five-fold ministries, that ministry is 4th in your life.

**2 Thessalonians 3:10**
*For even when we were with you, this we commanded you, that **if any would not work, neither should he eat.***

**WORK TO PROVIDE**
If you are not called to one of the five-fold ministries of the Church, your work to provide for your family is 4th priority.

## V. Local Church Work and Attendance is 5th

**1 Corinthians 12:28**
*And God hath set some in the church, first apostles, secondarily prophets, thirdly teachers, after that miracles, then gifts of healings, helps, governments, diversities of tongues.*

You can both work in the local church and attend services in the local church.

*Priorities & Problem Prevention*

Workers in the church include Sunday School and other teachers, ushers, choir members, officers, secretaries and etc.

**Hebrews 10:25**
*Not forsaking the assembling of ourselves together, as the manner of some is; but exhorting one another.*

God is saying that we should assemble together as bodies of believers. It strengthens us.

### VI Favor the Husband's Family Before the Wife's Family

**Exodus 20:12**
*Honor thy father and thy mother: that thy days may be long upon the land which the LORD thy God giveth thee.*

You are to honor your parents all the days of your life. God promises your life will be long if you keep this commandment.

**Psalms 45:10**
*Hearken, O daughter, and consider, and incline thine ear;* **forget also thine own people, and thy father's house.**

When your wife leaves her father's household, she joins the household of her husband and gives favor to it.

### VII Favor Christians over Non Christians.

**1 Corinthians 16:15-16**
*15 ...And that they have addicted themselves to the* **ministry of the saints,)**

*16 That ye* **submit yourselves unto such...**

5

## Galatians 6:10
*As we have therefore opportunity, let us do good unto all men, **especially unto them who are of the household of faith.***

## Romans 12:10
*Be kindly affectioned one to another with brotherly love; in honour **preferring one another.***

God is saying that as we have the opportunity, we are to addict ourselves to serve others in the church.

## VIII Things Are Last

## Matthew 6:33
*But seek ye first the kingdom of God and his righteousness, and all these things shall be added unto you.*

I want you to know why God says this. The main reason is that he wants your heart.

## Luke 12:34
*For where your treasure is, there will your heart be also.*

He wants you to have things; but he does not want things to have you.

Solomon got a good start in his life when he asked the LORD the following:

## 1 Kings 3:9
*Give therefore thy servant an understanding heart to judge thy people...*

*Priorities & Problem Prevention*

And God, being pleased by what Solomon said from his heart, said the following:

**1 Kings 3:11**
*11 Because thou hast asked this thing, and hast not asked for thyself long life; neither has asked riches for thyself...*

*13 ...And I have also given thee that which thou hast not asked, both riches, and honour..."*

And God delivered not only to Solomon but the people as well. The scriptures tell us:

**2 Chronicles 1:15**
*And the king made silver and gold at Jerusalem as plenteous as stones...*

And He will do the same thing for you and your household if you seek him first.

When all is said and done, if a course of action is not clear from scripture directly, you must consult God in prayer.

Consult God In Prayer

**Philippians 4:6**
*6 Be careful for nothing; but in every thing by prayer and supplication with thanksgiving let your requests be made known unto God.*

*Pre-Marriage Lesson #5*

*7 And the peace of God, which passeth all understanding, shall keep your hearts and minds through Christ Jesus.*

That wee small voice will tell you what to do. The more of God's word in your spirit, the louder and clearer that voice will sound to you.

*Priorities & Problem Prevention*

## Scriptural References for Pre-Marriage Lesson No. 5
(You may reproduce this list for your son or daughter.)

**God is first**
Mt 6:31 no thought, what shall we eat...drink...be clothed?
Mt 6:32 Father knoweth that ye have need of all these things.
Mt 6:33 seek ye first the kingdom of God...these things shall...

**Your wife (spouse) is second**
Eph 5:23 the husband is the head of the wife, even as Christ...
Eph 5:28 He that loveth his wife loveth himself.

**Your children are third**
1 Tim 3:4 ruleth his own house ... his children in subjection.
1 Tim 3:5 now how to rule his own house, how shall he take care...

**Work is fourth**
Eph 4:1 ye walk worthy of the vocation wherewith ye are called.
Eph 4:11 apostles...prophets...evangelists...pastors...teachers...
2 Thes 3:10 if any would not work, neither should he eat.

**Local Church work and attendance is fifth**
1 Cor 12:28 after that miracles...helps, governments...
Heb 10:25 Not forsaking the assembling of ourselves together...

**Favor the husband's family before the wife's family**
Exo 20:12 Honor thy father and thy mother: that thy days may be...
Psl 45:10 daughter...forget also ... thy father's house...

**Favor Christians over non-Christians**
1 Cor 16:15 addicted themselves to the ministry of the saints.
1 Cor 16:15 That ye submit yourselves unto such...
Gal 6:10 do good...especially unto...the household of faith.
Rom 12:12 kindly affectioned...preferring one another.

**Things are last**
Mt 6:33 seek...God..these things shall be added unto you.
Lk 12:34 where your treasure is there will your heart be also.
1 Kg 3:9 Give therefore thy servant an understanding heart...
1 Kg 3:11 Because..thou has not asked for thyself...
1 Kg 3:13 I have also given thee that which thou has not asked...
1 Chr 1:15 silver and gold at Jerusalem as plenteous as stones...

**Consult God in prayer**
Phil 4:6 Be careful for nothing...by prayer..let your requests...
Phil 4:7 And the peace of God, which passeth all understanding.

# How To Follow God's Map
## An Illustration of how to seek God first.

## H S — M A P

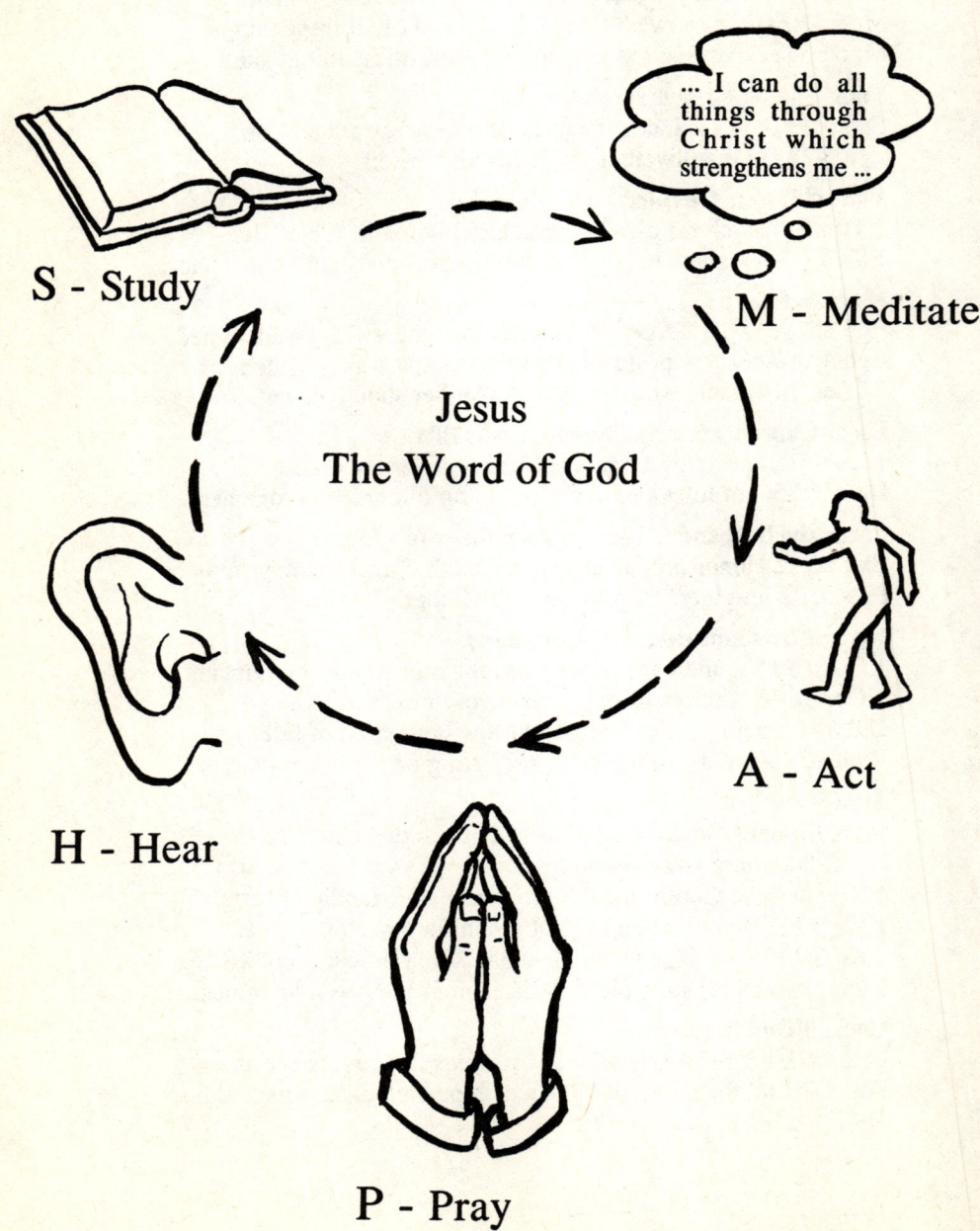

*Overview*
*Pre-Marriage Lesson No. 6*

# How to Follow God's Map

(This lesson is also taught as Sex Lesson No. 6.)

---

The scriptures tell us that:

Without faith it is impossible to please God: for he that cometh to God must believe that he is and that he is a rewarder of them that diligently seek him. (Hebrews 11:4)

And since he rewards those who diligently seek him, I am going to tell you how to seek him. In essence, you have to H-S-M-A-P which means to

H - Hear His Word
S - Study His Word
M - Meditate On His Word
A - Act On His Word
P - Pray Without Ceasing

Another way to remember this is to call it "His Map" without the "I" for Hear, Study, Meditate, Act and Pray, as shown in the sketch (opposite page).

When you and your wife put Jesus in the center of your marriage, you will be successful. Then Jesus is the head of your house and you are His undershepherd.

*Pre-Marriage Lesson #6*

## H  Hear His Word

**Hebrew 11:6**
*But without faith it is impossible to please him: for he that cometh to God must believe that he is, and that he is a rewarder of them that diligently seek him.*

You must hear his word. (Notice the part about rewards).

Faith is the word of God.

**Romans 10:17**
*So then faith cometh by **hearing**, and hearing by the word of God.*

You can hear the word at church, from audio tapes, radio, televisions, and etc.

## S  Study His Word

**2 Timothy 2:15**
***Study** to shew thyself approved unto God, a workman that needeth not to be ashamed, rightly dividing the word of truth.*

You can study God's word at Church, at home or in certain schools.

## M  Meditate On His Word

**Joshua 1:8**
*This book of the law shall not depart out of thy mouth; but **thou shalt meditate therein day and night**, that thou mayest observe and do according to all that is written therein: for then thou shalt*

make thy way prosperous, and then thou shalt have good success.

Notice that God's promise of prosperity and good success is the same as the things promised in Matthew 6:33 that we covered just a bit earlier.

## A Act On His Word

**James 1:22**
*But be ye **doers of the word,** and not hearers only, deceiving your own selves.*

This scripture is similar to Joshua 1:8 that we just talked about. In Joshua God says to 'observe and do.'

You act on God's word in everything that you do, whether it is loving your wife, chastising your children, working in a ministry or on a job, getting healed or etc.

A right relationship with God requires participation, not just observation.

## P Pray Without Ceasing

**1 Thessalonians 5:17**
*Pray without ceasing.*

**Ephesians 5:19**
*Speaking to yourselves in psalms and hymns and spiritual songs, singing and making melody in your heart to the Lord.*

Your relationship with God is one on one. You meet him in prayer. And the more of his words you know, the more you will understand of the small quiet voice he answers with.

*Pre-Marriage Lesson #6*

## Success In Life

Even when you cannot be in a private place to pray to God aloud, you can pray to him in word or song. Sometimes it can just be a song in your heart.

When your life is God centered, it will be successful.

Just as the power is delivered to a merry go 'round at its center pole, so is the power in your life delivered through Jesus Christ when he is the center of your life.

It may look fast and dazzling in the world of things, but the power is in the name of Jesus.

## Scriptural References for Pre-Marriage Lesson No. 6
(You may reproduce this list for your son or daughter)

**How to seek God (Hear, Study, Meditate, Act, Pray)**
Heb 11:6 without faith it is impossible to please Him...
Rom 10:17 faith cometh by hearing, and hearing by the word...
2 Tim 2:15 study to shew thyself approved unto God.
Jos 1:8 meditate therein day and night, ...thy way prosperous.
Jas 1:22 But be ye doers of the word, and not hearers only...
1 Thes 5:17 Pray without ceasing.
Eph 5:19 in psalms and hymns and spiritual...in your heart to...

*Overview*
*Pre-Marriage Lesson No. 7*

# Communications & Problem Solving

I want you to know that no matter how much you and your wife love each other, you will have problems. And when they come up, you should count it all joy as the scriptures say:

**James 1:2-3**
*2 My brethren, count it all joy when ye fall into divers temptations;*

*3 Knowing this, that the trying (proving) of your* **faith** *worketh patience.*

When these problems come up your faith must already be in action. As a result, you will develop greater and greater patience as you overcome the problems.

You and your wife, however must be in agreement for your marriage to be successful. As it is written:

**Amos 3:3**
*Can two walk together, except they be agreed?*

And the way you get into agreement is by communicating. If you don't say you agree, there is probably no agreement.

## Pre-Marriage Lesson #7

In this lesson we are going to cover seven communications principles from the scriptures. As you make them a part of your life, they will strengthen your marriage especially when you go through these trials.

**These principles are profitable for all communications in your life.**

The principles are as follows:

1. Speaking the truth in love
2. Being swift to hear, slow to speak, slow to anger
3. Reconcile differences
4. Speak no evil of each other
5. Speech seasoned with salt
6. No harsh communications out of your mouth
7. No anger by evening

In the end, as the head of the house you as the husband are ultimately responsible for whatever decisions are made in your family whether you, your wife or your children make the decisions.

Just as the head of state of a government is ultimately responsible for what the government does, you are responsible for your family. And you are responsible to God.

### Principle No. 1 — Speaking the Truth In Love.

**Ephesians 4:15**
*But speaking the truth in love, may grow up into him in all things, which is the head, even Christ.*

Speak the truth in love about all things, including:

- The satisfaction of sex
- The taste of the food
- Concern about body odor

*Communications & Problem Solving*

- Behavior of In-laws
- New hair style, beard
- Spouse driving habits
- Concern about tidiness
- Attention given to spouse
- Attention given to children
- Taking a new job
- Moving to another house
- Having house guests
- Vacation plans
- Newspaper reading at meals
- Unwelcome visitors
- What's wrong?

'In love' means:
    (See 1 Corinthians 13)

- In private/not public
- With patience
- With kindness
- With caring
- With tender affection
- With suggestions for change
- Without envy
- Without puffed up pride
- Without provocation
- Without ulterior motive

Notes:
_____
_____
_____
_____
_____

*Pre-Marriage Lesson #7*

---

### Principle No. 2
### Swift to Hear, Slow to Speak, Slow to Anger

**James 1:9**
*Wherefore, my beloved brethren, let every man be **swift to hear, slow to speak, slow to wrath**, for the wrath of man worketh not the righteousness of God.*

**Proverbs 14:17**
*He that is soon angry dealeth foolishly...*

Both you and your wife are to listen to each other very carefully. Then you are to speak **measured words** only after considering what the other has said.

If you get angry quickly, you are subject to act a fool.

---

### Principle No. 3
### Reconcile Differences

**2 Corinthians 5:18**
*Who hath reconciled us to himself by Jesus Christ, and hath given to us the ministry of reconciliation.*

**Proverbs 16:18**
*Pride goeth before destruction, and an haughty spirit before a fall.*

Jesus reconciled man to God. You and your wife must reconcile your differences too.

Remember, if you find you are wrong, admit it. If she admits error, accept it and forget it. Pride precedes destruction.

## Principle No. 4
### Speak No Evil Of Each Other

**James 4:11**
*Speak not evil one of another, brethren.*

Do not talk negatively about your wife **to anyone**. She should not tear you down either.

(If something really concerns you, 'Speak the truth in love, to her, not others!)

The two of you are one flesh. **Speaking evil of her is speaking evil of yourself.**

## Principle No. 5
### Speech Seasoned With Salt

**Colossians 4:6**
*Let your speech be always with grace, seasoned with salt, that ye may know how ye ought to answer every man.*

Your words should be seasoned with love, even when you and your wife disagree. Honor her as the weaker vessel. (Both of you are vessels.)

Notes:
_____
_____
_____
_____

*Pre-Marriage Lesson #7*

## Principle No. 6
### No Corrupt Communications

**Ephesians 4:29**
*Let no corrupt communication proceed out of your mouth, but that which is good to the use of edifying, that it may minister grace unto the hearers.*

No harsh words should come out of your mouth. All of your words should build your wife up, not tear her down.

## Principle No. 7
### No Sundown on Wrath

**Ephesians 4:26-27**
*26 Be ye angry, and sin not: let not the sun go down upon your wrath:*

*27 Neither give place to the devil.*

**Genesis 4:6-7**
*6 And the LORD said unto Cain, 'Why art thou wroth? And why is thy countenance fallen?'*

*7 If thou doest well, shalt thou not be accepted? And if thou doest not well, SIN lieth at the door.'*

In Ephesians, God is saying not to let the sun go down and find you angry, otherwise the devil can do his evil work.

In Genesis, God warns Cain not to be angry because SIN (the devil) was just waiting to take control of him.

Closing Note:
Son, you are the head of your house as Christ is the head of the church. Just remember that he wants your wife to obey you as you obey him. Your leadership is in the Lord.

Notes:
_____

_____

## Scriptural References for Pre-Marriage Lesson No. 7
(You may reproduce this list for your son or daughter)

**Lesson Overview**
Jas 1:2 count it all joy when ye fall into divers temptations...
Jas 1:3 knowing this...trying of your faith worketh patience.
Amos 3:3 Can two walk together, except they agree?
1 Pet 3:7 according to knowledge...honour...the weaker vessel...
1 Cor 7:5 Defraud ye not one the other.

**Principle No. 1**
Eph 4:15 But speaking the truth in love, may grow up into him...
1 Cor 13 [the entire chapter]

**Principle No. 2**
Jas 1:9 be swift to hear, slow to speak, slow to wrath...
Prov 14:17 He that is soon angry dealeth foolishly...

**Principle No. 3**
2 Cor 5:18 and hath given to us the ministry of reconciliation...

**Principle No. 4**
Jas 4:11 Speak not evil one of another, brethren.

**Principle No. 5**
Col 4:6 speech be always with grace, seasoned with salt...

**Principle No. 6**
Eph 4:29 no corrupt communications proceed out of your mouth...

**Principle No. 7**
Eph 4:26 let not the sun go down upon your wrath...
Eph 4:27 Neither give place to the devil.
Gen 4:6 Why art thou wroth?..thy countenance fallen?
Gen 4:7 Sin lieth at the door.

*Closing Comments*
*Pre-Marriage Lessons*

# A Marriage With Vision

**Proverbs 29:18**
*Where there is no vision, the people perish.*

---

**The Most Important Vision**
Without a vision, your marriage will perish, too! And one of the most important visions for your marriage is that of Jesus at his second coming. As Hebrews 9:28 says:

> *"...Unto them that look for him (Jesus) shall he appear the second time without sin unto salvation."*

**The Need to Pray Together**
You and your wife should pray together, especially when you need to be in agreement about the same things. Jesus said this in Matthew:

> **Matthew 18:19**
> *...That if two of you shall agree on earth as touching anything that they shall ask, it shall be done for them of my Father which is in heaven.*

*A Marriage With Vision*

**The Pre-Marital Visions**
Before you get married, you should agree on an initial set of spiritually based visions for your marriage (such as further education and having children). If you do not agree before marriage, you should not marry each other. The Scriptures say:

**Amos 3:3**
*Can two walk together, except they be agreed?*

**A Maturing Marriage**
You should read these lessons together and discuss them at least once a year during your marriage. (Perhaps during the month leading up to your wedding anniversary.) For scriptures that seem especially timely for love reinforcement as well as correction, I suggest you read them aloud to each other.

By doing all of the things included in these lessons, your marriage will be very successful.